I0012502

Data Science and Python

Data Science and Web Development with Flask

From Machine Learning to Deployment

Python

MARK JOHN LADO

DEDICATION

This book is dedicated to the aspiring data scientists and web developers who dare to bridge the gap between insightful analysis and impactful applications. It is for those who believe in the power of data to transform the world and who seek the practical skills to bring their visions to life. May this book serve as a guide on your journey, illuminating the path from raw data to deployed solution.

I hope it sparks curiosity, fuels your passion, and empowers you to build innovative and data-driven web applications. This work is also dedicated to the open-source community, whose tireless efforts have made the tools and technologies explored here freely accessible.

ACKNOWLEDGMENTS

I extend my sincere gratitude to everyone who contributed to the creation of this book.

First and foremost, I thank my family and friends for their unwavering support and encouragement throughout this project. Their patience and understanding were invaluable. I am deeply grateful to the reviewers whose insightful feedback significantly improved the quality and clarity of the content.

I also acknowledge the creators and maintainers of the open-source libraries that form the foundation of this book, including NumPy, Pandas, Matplotlib, Scikit-learn, Flask, TensorFlow, and Keras. Their dedication to building powerful and accessible tools has made this work possible.

Finally, I thank the publishing team for their guidance and expertise in bringing this book to fruition.

Table of Contents

Part 1 Foundations of Data Science and Python

Chapter 1 Introduction to Data Science

What is Data Science?

Data Science is an interdisciplinary field that combines statistical analysis, machine learning, and domain expertise to extract meaningful insights from data. In today's data-driven world, organizations across industries rely on data science to make informed decisions, optimize processes, and predict future trends. For instance, Netflix uses data science to recommend personalized content to its users, while healthcare providers leverage predictive models to diagnose diseases early (Provost & Fawcett, 2013). The field's versatility makes it a critical skill for computer science students and professionals alike.

A common question from beginners is, "What exactly does a data scientist do?" A data scientist's role involves collecting, cleaning, and analyzing data to uncover patterns and build predictive models. For example, a retail company might use data science to analyze customer purchase behavior and predict which products will sell best during a holiday season. This process often involves working with large datasets, which can be structured (e.g., CSV files, databases) or unstructured (e.g., text, images). Tools like Python, R, and SQL are essential for handling these tasks efficiently.

Another frequent concern is, "How do I get started with data science?" The first step is to understand the data science workflow, which typically includes problem definition, data collection, data preprocessing, model building, evaluation, and deployment. For instance, if a student wants to predict student performance based on study habits, they would start by defining the problem, collecting data (e.g., hours studied, grades), cleaning the data (e.g., handling missing values), and then applying machine learning algorithms to build a predictive model. Python is particularly well-suited for this workflow due to its extensive libraries like Pandas for data manipulation, Matplotlib for visualization, and Scikit-learn for machine learning.

A potential challenge for beginners is the overwhelming amount of information available. To address this, it's important to focus on foundational concepts before diving into advanced topics. For example, understanding basic statistics and probability is crucial for interpreting machine learning results. Additionally, hands-on practice with real-world datasets, such as those available on Kaggle or the UCI Machine Learning Repository, can help solidify these concepts. Educators can facilitate this by incorporating project-based learning into their curriculum, where students work on end-to-end data science projects.

In conclusion, data science is a powerful tool for solving real-world problems, and its applications are vast and growing. By starting with a strong foundation in Python and the data science workflow, students can build the skills needed to tackle complex challenges. As they progress, they can explore advanced topics like deep learning and big data analytics, further expanding their expertise. For educators, emphasizing practical applications and providing access to real-world datasets can enhance student engagement and learning outcomes.

Applications of Data Science

Data science has become a transformative force across industries, enabling organizations to harness the power of data for decision-making, innovation, and efficiency. One of the most prominent applications of data science is in the field of healthcare, where predictive models are used to diagnose diseases, personalize treatment plans, and optimize hospital operations. For example, IBM's Watson Health leverages machine learning algorithms to analyze medical records and suggest treatment options for cancer patients (Ramesh et al., 2004). This not only improves patient outcomes but also reduces the burden on healthcare providers. However, a common question arises: "How can data science handle the complexity and variability of medical data?" The answer lies in robust data preprocessing techniques, such as handling missing values and normalizing data, combined with advanced algorithms like neural networks that can capture intricate patterns in large datasets.

Another significant application is in the retail and e-commerce sector, where data science drives customer segmentation, demand forecasting, and personalized marketing. Amazon, for instance, uses recommendation systems powered by collaborative filtering and deep learning to suggest products to users based on their browsing and purchase history (Linden et al., 2003). This not only enhances the customer experience but also boosts sales. A challenge often faced by students is understanding how to build such recommendation systems. The solution involves starting with simpler algorithms like matrix factorization and gradually progressing to more complex models like neural networks, while ensuring the data is clean and well-structured.

In the realm of finance, data science plays a critical role in fraud detection, risk management, and algorithmic trading. For example, credit card companies use anomaly detection algorithms to identify fraudulent transactions in real time (Bolton & Hand, 2002). This requires analyzing vast amounts of transactional data and identifying patterns that deviate from the norm. A question that frequently arises is, "How can we ensure the accuracy of these models?" This can be addressed by using techniques like cross-validation and ensemble methods, which improve model robustness and reduce the risk of overfitting.

The transportation and logistics industry also benefits immensely from data science. Companies like Uber and FedEx use predictive analytics to optimize routes, reduce delivery times, and minimize fuel consumption. For instance, Uber's surge pricing algorithm dynamically adjusts prices based on demand and supply, ensuring efficient allocation of resources (Chen et al., 2015). A common concern among students is, "How do we handle real-time data processing in such applications?" This can be tackled by leveraging distributed computing frameworks like Apache Spark and streaming platforms like Apache Kafka, which enable real-time data analysis at scale.

In social media and entertainment, data science is used for sentiment analysis, content recommendation, and user engagement. Platforms like Netflix and Spotify analyze user behavior to recommend movies, shows, and music tailored to individual preferences (Gomez-Uribe & Hunt, 2015). A challenge here is dealing with unstructured data, such as text and audio. Practical solutions include using natural language processing (NLP) techniques for text analysis and deep learning models for audio and image processing.

Despite its widespread applications, data science is not without challenges. One major issue is the ethical use of data, particularly in terms of privacy and bias. For example, facial recognition systems have been criticized for exhibiting racial bias (Buolamwini & Gebru, 2018). To address this, it is essential to incorporate fairness and transparency into the design of data science models, ensuring they are both accurate and equitable.

In conclusion, the applications of data science are vast and impactful, spanning healthcare, retail, finance, transportation, and entertainment. By understanding these real-world use cases, students can appreciate the practical relevance of data science and its potential to solve complex problems. Educators can enhance learning by incorporating case studies and hands-on projects that simulate real-world scenarios, enabling students to apply theoretical knowledge to practical challenges. As the field continues to evolve, staying updated with the latest tools and techniques will be crucial for both students and professionals.

Data Science Workflow

The data science workflow is a structured process that guides data scientists from problem definition to the deployment of solutions. It serves as a roadmap for tackling complex data-driven challenges and ensures that projects are executed systematically and efficiently. A common question from students is, "Why is a structured workflow necessary?" The answer lies in the complexity of data science projects, which often involve large datasets, multiple stakeholders, and iterative processes. Without a clear workflow, projects can become disorganized, leading to inefficiencies and suboptimal results. For example, in a real-world scenario like predicting customer churn for a telecom company, skipping the data preprocessing step could result in inaccurate models due to missing or inconsistent data (Kelleher et al., 2015).

The first step in the data science workflow is problem definition, where the goal is to clearly articulate the business problem and the objectives of the analysis. For instance, a retail company might want to predict which customers are likely to purchase a new product. This step involves collaborating with stakeholders to understand their needs and defining key performance indicators (KPIs) to measure success. A common challenge here is ensuring that the problem is neither too broad nor too narrow. Educators can guide students by encouraging them to break down complex problems into smaller, manageable tasks and to use frameworks like SMART (Specific, Measurable, Achievable, Relevant, Time-bound) to define objectives.

The next step is data collection, where relevant data is gathered from various sources, such as databases, APIs, or web scraping. In the telecom churn example, this might involve collecting customer demographics, usage patterns, and billing information. A frequent question is, "How do we ensure the quality of the data?" Practical solutions include validating data sources, checking for completeness, and documenting the data collection process to ensure reproducibility. Tools like Python's Pandas library can be used to load and inspect datasets, while APIs like Twitter's or Google's can facilitate access to real-time data.

Once the data is collected, the data preprocessing step involves cleaning and transforming the data to make it suitable for analysis. This includes handling missing values, removing duplicates, and encoding categorical variables. For example, in a healthcare dataset, missing patient records might be imputed using statistical methods, while text data like doctor's notes might be tokenized for NLP applications. A common challenge is dealing with noisy or inconsistent data. Educators can teach students techniques like outlier detection and normalization, as well as the importance of documenting preprocessing steps to maintain transparency.

The exploratory data analysis (EDA) phase is where data scientists uncover patterns, trends, and relationships in the data. Visualization tools like Matplotlib and Seaborn in Python are invaluable for this step. For instance, a scatter plot might reveal a correlation between customer age and product preference in a retail dataset. A question often asked is, "How do we interpret these visualizations?" The key is to combine statistical analysis with domain knowledge to draw meaningful insights. Educators can emphasize the importance of asking the right questions during EDA, such as "What factors influence customer churn?" or "Are there seasonal trends in sales data?"

After EDA, the model building step involves selecting and training machine learning algorithms. For example, a logistic regression model might be used to predict customer churn, while a decision tree could classify email spam. A common challenge is choosing the right algorithm for the problem. Practical solutions include starting with simpler models like linear regression or k-nearest neighbors (KNN) and gradually moving to more complex models like random forests or neural networks. Cross-validation techniques can help evaluate model performance and prevent overfitting.

The model evaluation step ensures that the model performs well on unseen data. Metrics like accuracy, precision, recall, and F1-score are used to assess classification models, while mean squared error (MSE) and R-squared are common for regression models. In the telecom churn example, a high recall score might be prioritized to ensure that most churn cases are identified. A frequent question is, "What if the model performs poorly?" This can be addressed by revisiting earlier steps, such as feature engineering or hyperparameter tuning, and iterating on the model.

Finally, the deployment step involves integrating the model into a production environment, such as a web application or a mobile app. For instance, a Flask-based web app could allow users to input customer data and receive churn predictions in real time. A common challenge is ensuring that the model performs consistently in production. Solutions include monitoring model performance, updating the model with new data, and using containerization tools like Docker to ensure reproducibility.

In conclusion, the data science workflow is a critical framework for solving real-world problems systematically. By following this structured approach, students can develop the skills needed to tackle complex data science projects and deliver actionable insights. Educators can enhance learning by incorporating real-world case studies and hands-on projects that simulate the entire workflow, from problem definition to deployment. As the field of data science continues to evolve, mastering this workflow will remain essential for both students and professionals.

Tools and Libraries for Data Science (NumPy, Pandas, Matplotlib, Scikit-learn)

The success of a data science project often hinges on the tools and libraries used to manipulate, analyze, and visualize data. Python, with its rich ecosystem of libraries, has emerged as the lingua franca of data science due to its simplicity, versatility, and extensive community support. Among the most essential libraries are NumPy, Pandas, Matplotlib, and Scikit-learn, each serving a distinct purpose in the data science workflow. A common question from students is, "Why are these libraries so widely adopted, and how do they complement each other?" The answer lies in their specialized functionalities, which, when combined, provide a comprehensive toolkit for tackling data science challenges.

NumPy (Numerical Python) is the foundation for numerical computing in Python. It provides support for arrays, matrices, and mathematical functions, making it indispensable for tasks that involve heavy numerical computations. For example, in a real-world scenario like simulating the spread of a virus, NumPy can be used to perform matrix operations that model population interactions (Harris et al., 2020). A frequent challenge for beginners is understanding the concept of vectorization, which allows operations to be performed on entire arrays without explicit loops. Educators can address this by demonstrating how vectorized operations in NumPy are not only more concise but also significantly faster than traditional loops, especially for large datasets.

Pandas builds on NumPy by providing high-level data structures like DataFrames, which are ideal for handling structured data. In a retail setting, for instance, Pandas can be used to analyze sales data stored in CSV files, enabling tasks like filtering, grouping, and aggregating data with just a few lines of code. A common question is, "How do I handle missing or inconsistent data in Pandas?" Practical solutions include using methods like dropna() to remove missing values or fillna() to impute them, as well as leveraging the apply() function for custom data transformations. Educators can emphasize the importance of data cleaning and preprocessing, as these steps often consume a significant portion of a data scientist's time.

Matplotlib is the go-to library for data visualization in Python. It allows users to create a wide range of static, animated, and interactive plots, from simple line charts to complex heatmaps. For example, in a financial analysis project, Matplotlib can be used to visualize stock price trends over time, helping analysts identify patterns and make informed decisions. A frequent challenge is creating publication-quality visualizations that are both informative and aesthetically pleasing. Educators can teach students to customize plots by adjusting colors, labels, and annotations, as well as to use libraries like Seaborn, which builds on Matplotlib to provide higher-level interfaces for statistical graphics.

Scikit-learn is the cornerstone of machine learning in Python, offering a unified interface for implementing a wide range of algorithms, from linear regression to support vector machines. In a healthcare application, for instance, Scikit-learn can be used to build a model that predicts patient readmission rates based on historical data. A common question is, "How do I choose the right algorithm for my problem?" The answer lies in understanding the nature of the data and the problem at hand. For example, classification problems like spam detection might require algorithms like logistic regression or random forests, while clustering tasks like customer segmentation might call for k-means or hierarchical clustering. Educators can guide students through the process of model selection, evaluation, and tuning, emphasizing the importance of cross-validation and hyperparameter optimization.

A recurring concern among students is the steep learning curve associated with these libraries. To address this, educators can adopt a hands-on approach, using real-world datasets and step-by-step tutorials to demonstrate the practical applications of each library. For instance, a project analyzing Airbnb listings could involve using Pandas for data cleaning, Matplotlib for visualizing price distributions, and Scikit-learn for predicting booking rates. By working on such projects, students can gain a deeper understanding of how these tools integrate into the broader data science workflow.

In conclusion, NumPy, Pandas, Matplotlib, and Scikit-learn form the backbone of data science in Python, each contributing unique capabilities that are essential for solving real-world problems. By mastering these tools, students can develop the technical skills needed to manipulate, analyze, and visualize data, as well as build and evaluate machine learning models. Educators play a crucial role in bridging the gap between theory and practice, ensuring that students are not only familiar with these libraries but also proficient in applying them to real-world scenarios. As the field of data science continues to evolve, staying updated with the latest developments in these tools will remain critical for both students and professionals.

Chapter 2 Python for Data Science

Python Basics (Variables, Data Types, Control Structures)

Let's delve into the foundational building blocks of Python for data science, focusing on variables, data types, and control structures. These elements are crucial, forming the bedrock upon which more complex data manipulation and analysis are built. Imagine you're tasked with analyzing a dataset of customer purchase history for an e-commerce platform. You'll likely encounter various data types: customer IDs (integers), product prices (floats), purchase dates (strings or datetime objects), and customer demographics (often categorical data represented as strings). Python's dynamic typing allows you to easily assign these different data types to variables without explicit declarations, making it flexible for handling diverse datasets. For example, customer_id = 12345 assigns an integer to customer_id, while price = 29.99 assigns a float to price. However, understanding the nuances of these types is essential. A common pitfall is attempting arithmetic operations on strings when numeric types are expected. If you accidentally try to add "10" and "20" as strings, you'll get "1020" (concatenation) instead of 30 (addition). This highlights the importance of type checking and conversion using functions like int() or float(). Control structures, such as if-else statements and loops, are equally vital. Suppose you need to categorize customers based on their total spending. An if-else structure can determine if a customer qualifies as "high-value" based on a threshold: if total_spending > 1000: customer_category = "high-value" else: customer_category = "regular". Loops, like for and while, are indispensable for iterating through datasets. Imagine calculating the average purchase value for each customer. A for loop could iterate through a list of customer purchases, accumulating the total spending for each customer before calculating the average. Furthermore, list comprehensions, a concise way to create lists, can significantly improve code readability and efficiency. For instance, squared_prices = [price**2 for price in prices] efficiently calculates the square of each price in a list. As you progress into more advanced data science techniques, a solid grasp of these fundamental concepts will prove invaluable. A strong foundation in Python's core elements, as discussed by experts like Beazley (2013) in the Python Essential Reference, is crucial before tackling more complex topics. What if a student struggles with the concept of data type conversion? A practical exercise involving a real-world dataset, like converting string representations of dates into datetime objects for time series analysis, can solidify their understanding. Another common question arises regarding the efficiency of different looping methods. Discussing the relative performance of for loops, while loops, and list comprehensions with examples, perhaps referencing the performance tips outlined in the official Python documentation, can provide practical guidance. By understanding the core principles and practicing with real-world scenarios, students can effectively leverage Python for data science tasks.

Working with Libraries (NumPy, Pandas, Matplotlib)

The power of Python for data science truly shines when we leverage its rich ecosystem of libraries, particularly NumPy, Pandas, and Matplotlib. These libraries provide specialized tools that drastically simplify complex data manipulation, analysis, and visualization tasks. NumPy, the cornerstone of numerical computing in Python, introduces the ndarray, a powerful N-dimensional array object. Imagine you're working with image data, where each image is represented as a grid of pixel values. NumPy arrays provide an efficient way to store and manipulate these pixel values, enabling operations like image resizing, filtering, and feature extraction. Instead of iterating through individual pixels using nested loops (which can be computationally expensive), NumPy allows you to perform operations on entire arrays at once, significantly boosting performance. For instance, calculating the mean pixel value across all images in a dataset becomes a single, concise NumPy operation. As McKinney (2012) explains in his seminal work on data analysis with Python, NumPy's vectorized operations are a key reason for Python's popularity in scientific computing. A common question students often ask is why NumPy arrays are more efficient than standard Python lists. The answer lies in NumPy's contiguous memory allocation and optimized C implementations, enabling faster access and manipulation of array elements.

Pandas builds upon NumPy by providing high-level data structures like Series (one-dimensional labeled arrays) and DataFrames (two-dimensional labeled tables). These structures are tailor-made for working with tabular data, which is ubiquitous in data science. Consider a dataset containing sales transactions, with columns for product ID, customer ID, purchase date, and amount. Pandas DataFrames allow you to easily load, clean, transform, and analyze this data. You can perform operations like filtering transactions based on specific criteria (e.g., finding all transactions above a certain amount), grouping transactions by customer ID to calculate total spending, or joining data from different sources. Pandas also handles missing data gracefully, providing methods for imputation or removal. Furthermore, Pandas integrates seamlessly with other libraries, making it a central hub for data manipulation within the Python data science workflow. A practical example could involve analyzing website traffic data, where Pandas can be used to clean and aggregate user activity logs, enabling insights into user behavior and website performance. Students often struggle with the concept of indexing and selecting data within Pandas DataFrames. Providing clear examples with different indexing methods (.loc, .iloc, etc.) and emphasizing the distinction between label-based and integer-based indexing can help clarify this concept.

Matplotlib, the plotting library, allows you to create a wide variety of visualizations, from simple scatter plots and line charts to more complex heatmaps and 3D plots. Visualizations are crucial for exploring data, communicating insights, and presenting results. Imagine you've analyzed the sales transaction data using Pandas and want to visualize the distribution of customer spending. Matplotlib enables you to create histograms, box plots, or other relevant charts to represent this distribution. Visualizations can reveal patterns and trends that might not be immediately apparent from raw data, facilitating a deeper understanding of the underlying phenomena. Seaborn, built on top of Matplotlib, provides a higher-level interface for creating statistically informative and visually appealing plots. For example, Seaborn's pairplot function can quickly generate a matrix of scatter plots showing the relationships between multiple variables in a dataset. A common challenge for beginners is choosing the appropriate type of visualization for a given dataset and task. Guiding students through examples of different plot types and explaining their strengths and weaknesses, perhaps referencing the work of Wilkinson (2005) on the grammar of graphics, can improve their ability to create effective visualizations. By mastering NumPy, Pandas, and Matplotlib, students equip themselves with the essential tools for tackling real-world data science problems, from data cleaning and preprocessing to statistical analysis and visualization.

Data Manipulation with Pandas

Pandas, a cornerstone of the Python data science ecosystem, empowers us with highly efficient tools for data manipulation. Its strength lies in its DataFrame object, a two-dimensional labeled data structure that resembles a table in a relational database or a spreadsheet. Imagine you're dealing with a dataset of sensor readings from a network of IoT devices. Each reading might include a timestamp, sensor ID, temperature, humidity, and location. Pandas allows you to load this data from various sources (CSV, JSON, SQL databases, etc.) into a DataFrame, making it readily available for analysis. A key strength of Pandas is its ability to handle heterogeneous data, meaning that different columns in the DataFrame can hold different data types (e.g., timestamps, integers, floats, strings). This is crucial for real-world datasets that often contain a mix of numerical and categorical information. As McKinney (2012) highlights, Pandas' flexible data structures and intuitive API significantly streamline the process of data wrangling, a critical step in any data science project.

One of the most frequent tasks in data manipulation is data cleaning. Real-world datasets are often messy, containing missing values, inconsistent formatting, and duplicate entries. Pandas provides powerful methods for addressing these issues. For instance, you can use fillna() to replace missing values with a specific value (e.g., the mean or median of the column) or dropna() to remove rows or columns containing missing values. Consider the sensor data example: some readings might be missing due to temporary network outages. Pandas allows you to impute these missing values based on the readings from neighboring sensors or using more sophisticated techniques. Another common cleaning task is handling inconsistent data formats. Suppose the timestamps in your dataset are stored as strings in different formats. Pandas provides functions like to_datetime() to convert these strings into a consistent datetime format, enabling time-based analysis. A question that often arises is how to choose the best strategy for handling missing data. The answer depends on the specific dataset and the goals of the analysis. Discussing the trade-offs between imputation and removal, and introducing techniques like forward fill or backward fill, can provide students with practical guidance.

Beyond data cleaning, Pandas provides a rich set of functionalities for data transformation. You can easily filter data based on specific conditions, select specific columns, sort data, group data by one or more columns, and perform aggregations (e.g., calculating the sum, mean, or standard deviation). Consider the sensor data again: you might want to analyze the temperature readings for a specific location or calculate the average humidity for each day. Pandas' groupby() method allows you to group the data by location or date and then apply aggregation functions to each group. Another powerful feature is data merging and joining, which allows you to combine data from multiple sources. Suppose you have additional information about the sensor locations, such as their latitude and longitude, stored in a separate file. Pandas' merge() or join() functions enable you to combine this information with the sensor readings based on the sensor ID. Students often find the concept of "joins" challenging, particularly the different types of joins (inner, outer, left, right). Visualizing these joins using diagrams and providing clear examples with real-world datasets can significantly improve their understanding. By mastering Pandas' data manipulation capabilities, data scientists can efficiently prepare and transform data for analysis, paving the way for meaningful insights and model building.

Data Visualization with Matplotlib and Seaborn

Data visualization is an indispensable tool in the data science toolkit, providing a powerful means to explore data, communicate insights, and guide decision-making. Matplotlib, a foundational plotting library in Python, serves as the bedrock for creating a wide array of static, interactive, and animated visualizations. Imagine you've conducted a survey collecting data on student demographics, academic performance, and extracurricular activities. Matplotlib allows you to create histograms to visualize the distribution of student ages, scatter plots to explore the relationship between study time and grades, or bar charts to compare participation rates in different extracurricular activities. As Hunter (2007) describes in the Matplotlib documentation, its object-oriented architecture provides fine-grained control over every aspect of a plot, from axis labels and titles to colors and line styles. This flexibility allows you to tailor visualizations to specific needs and ensure clarity in communication. A common question students often ask is how to choose the right type of plot for a given dataset. The answer depends on the nature of the data and the message you want to convey. Providing clear examples of different plot types (scatter plots for relationships, histograms for distributions, bar charts for comparisons, etc.) and discussing their strengths and weaknesses can help students make informed choices.

While Matplotlib offers extensive customization, creating visually appealing and statistically informative plots can sometimes require a significant amount of code. Seaborn, built on top of Matplotlib, addresses this by providing a high-level interface for creating aesthetically pleasing and statistically rich visualizations. Consider the student survey data again: you might want to visualize the relationship between multiple variables, such as study time, attendance, and grades, while also accounting for factors like gender or socioeconomic background. Seaborn's pairplot function can quickly generate a matrix of scatter plots showing the pairwise relationships between these variables, revealing potential correlations and patterns. Furthermore, Seaborn integrates seamlessly with Pandas DataFrames, making it easy to visualize data directly from your data manipulation workflows. Waskom et al. (2017) showcase Seaborn's capabilities in their publication, highlighting its ability to create complex statistical graphics with minimal code. One challenge that beginners often face is understanding the statistical interpretations of Seaborn's plots, such as confidence intervals or error bars. Explaining the underlying statistical concepts and providing clear interpretations of the visualizations can enhance their understanding.

Beyond basic plotting, both Matplotlib and Seaborn offer functionalities for creating more advanced visualizations. Matplotlib supports 3D plotting, allowing you to visualize data in three dimensions, which can be useful for exploring complex datasets. Seaborn provides specialized plot types for visualizing specific types of data, such as time series data or categorical data. For instance, Seaborn's lineplot function is ideal for visualizing trends in time series data, while boxplot or violinplot can effectively display the distribution of categorical data. Imagine you're analyzing stock market data: Matplotlib can be used to create 3D surface plots to visualize the price fluctuations of different stocks over time, while Seaborn's lineplot can be used to track the performance of a specific stock over a given period. A frequent question from students is how to customize the appearance of their plots, such as changing colors, fonts, or adding annotations. Demonstrating the various customization options available in both Matplotlib and Seaborn, and providing practical examples of how to apply these options, can empower students to create visually compelling and informative visualizations. By mastering Matplotlib and Seaborn, data scientists can effectively explore their data, communicate their findings, and gain valuable insights from their analyses.

Chapter 3 Data Preprocessing

Handling Missing Data

Handling missing data is a crucial step in any data science project. Real-world datasets are rarely perfect, often containing missing values due to various reasons, such as data entry errors, sensor malfunctions, or incomplete surveys. Ignoring missing data can lead to biased or inaccurate results, while inappropriate handling can introduce further distortions. Therefore, understanding different strategies for dealing with missing data is essential. A common scenario is analyzing customer purchase history where some customers might not have provided their age or income. These missing values need to be addressed before any meaningful analysis can be performed. As Little and Rubin (2019) discuss in their seminal work on statistical analysis with missing data, the choice of method depends heavily on the nature of the missing data mechanism.

The first step in handling missing data is identifying it. Pandas, a powerful Python library for data manipulation, provides functions like isnull() and isna() to detect missing values in a DataFrame. These functions return a boolean mask indicating the presence or absence of missing data. Imagine you have a dataset of patient records with missing blood pressure readings. You can use df.isnull().sum() to count the number of missing values in each column, quickly identifying which variables have the most missing data. Visualizing the missing data patterns using heatmaps or missingness maps can also be beneficial in understanding if the missingness is random or related to other variables. A common question is how to differentiate between different types of missing data mechanisms (Missing Completely At Random (MCAR), Missing At Random (MAR), and Not Missing At Random (NMAR)).[1] Explaining these mechanisms with real-world examples (e.g., MCAR - a sensor randomly fails to record data; MAR - older patients are less likely to provide income information; NMAR - patients with severe illness are less likely to report symptoms) is crucial for students to choose appropriate imputation strategies.

Once missing data is identified, several strategies can be employed. One straightforward approach is deletion. Rows or columns with missing values can be removed. However, this approach can lead to significant data loss if a substantial portion of the data is missing, potentially biasing the results. Suppose in the customer purchase history example, you simply delete all customers with missing age information. This could lead to a biased analysis if age is correlated with purchasing behavior. Another common strategy is imputation, where missing values are replaced with estimated values. Simple imputation techniques include filling missing values with the mean, median, or mode of the corresponding column. For numerical variables like blood pressure, the mean or median might be suitable, while for categorical variables like preferred communication method, the mode might be more appropriate. More sophisticated imputation methods include K-Nearest Neighbors (KNN) imputation, which imputes missing values based on the values of similar data points, and regression imputation, which uses regression models to predict missing values. A frequent question is when to use simple imputation versus more sophisticated techniques. The complexity of the imputation method should be balanced with the computational cost and the potential impact on the analysis. Simple imputation might be sufficient for small amounts of missing data, while more complex methods might be necessary for larger datasets or when the missing data is not MCAR.

Finally, it's crucial to evaluate the impact of missing data handling on the analysis results. Comparing the results obtained with different imputation methods or deletion strategies can help assess the robustness of the findings. Furthermore, it's essential to document the chosen strategy and its potential limitations transparently. For instance, if you used mean imputation for blood pressure, acknowledge that this might underestimate the variability in blood pressure. By carefully considering the nature of missing data, choosing appropriate handling strategies, and evaluating their impact, data scientists can ensure the validity and reliability of their analyses. Students often struggle with understanding the assumptions behind different imputation methods. Providing clear explanations and examples, perhaps using simulated datasets with known missing data mechanisms, can help them grasp these concepts and apply them effectively. Furthermore, emphasizing the importance of documenting the chosen strategy and its potential limitations promotes responsible data science practices.

Data Cleaning and Transformation

Data cleaning and transformation are essential, often time-consuming, steps in the data science pipeline. Real-world data is rarely pristine; it may contain inconsistencies, errors, and irrelevant information that can hinder analysis and model building. Imagine working with a dataset of customer reviews for a movie streaming service. You might encounter reviews with typos, inconsistent capitalization, HTML tags, or irrelevant information like timestamps. Data cleaning addresses these issues, ensuring data quality and consistency. Data transformation, on the other hand, involves converting data into a suitable format for analysis. This might involve scaling numerical features, encoding categorical variables, or creating new features from existing ones. As Wickham (2014) argues in his work on tidy data, a well-structured dataset is crucial for effective data analysis and visualization.

The first step in data cleaning is often identifying inconsistencies and errors. This might involve checking for duplicate entries, identifying outliers, or detecting incorrect data types. Pandas provides several useful functions for this purpose. For instance, duplicated() can identify duplicate rows, describe() provides summary statistics that can help detect outliers, and dtypes reveals the data type of each column. Consider the movie review example: you might use duplicated() to identify and remove duplicate reviews, or describe() to identify reviews with unusually high or low word counts, which could indicate errors. Regular expressions can be invaluable for identifying and cleaning up text data. For example, you could use a regular expression to remove HTML tags from the reviews or to standardize capitalization. A common question is how to distinguish between genuine outliers and errors in the data. Visualizing the data using box plots or scatter plots can be helpful in identifying outliers. Domain knowledge is also crucial in determining whether an outlier is a genuine extreme value or a data entry error.

Once inconsistencies and errors are identified, appropriate cleaning techniques can be applied. Duplicate rows can be removed using drop_duplicates(). Outliers can be handled by either removing them, replacing them with a reasonable value (e.g., the mean or median), or transforming them using techniques like log transformation. Incorrect data types can be corrected using type conversion functions like astype(). For the movie review data, you might use replace() to correct common spelling errors or strip() to remove leading or trailing whitespace. Data transformation often involves converting categorical variables into numerical representations that machine learning algorithms can understand.[1] One-hot encoding is a common technique for this purpose, where each category is represented by a binary vector. For example, if the movie genre is a categorical variable, one-hot encoding would create separate columns for each genre (e.g., "Action," "Comedy," "Drama"), with a value of 1 indicating that the movie belongs to that genre and 0 otherwise. Another common transformation is feature scaling, which involves scaling numerical features to a similar range. This can be important for algorithms that are sensitive to the scale of the input features, such as K-Nearest Neighbors or Support Vector Machines. Standardization (z-score normalization) and Min-Max scaling are two common feature scaling techniques. A frequent question is when to use one-hot encoding versus other encoding techniques like label encoding. One-hot encoding is generally preferred for nominal categorical variables (where there is no inherent order), while label encoding might be suitable for ordinal categorical variables (where there is an order).

Finally, it's essential to document all cleaning and transformation steps. This ensures reproducibility and helps others understand how the data was prepared. Consider creating a data dictionary that describes each variable, its data type, and any transformations that were applied. For the movie review data, you might document how you handled missing reviews, how you cleaned the text data, and how you encoded the movie genre. By carefully cleaning and transforming data, data scientists can ensure that their analyses are based on high-quality, consistent data, leading to more reliable and meaningful results. Students often struggle with deciding which cleaning or transformation technique is most appropriate for a given situation. Providing them with a range of examples and discussing the trade-offs between different techniques can help them develop their judgment in this crucial area. Furthermore, emphasizing the importance of documenting all steps promotes best practices in data science.

Feature Scaling and Normalization

Feature scaling and normalization are crucial preprocessing steps in machine learning, particularly when dealing with algorithms sensitive to the magnitude of input features. These techniques aim to transform numerical features into a similar range, preventing features with larger values from dominating the learning process and improving the performance of certain algorithms. Imagine you're building a model to predict house prices, and your dataset includes features like square footage (ranging from hundreds to thousands) and number of bedrooms (ranging from 1 to 5). Without scaling, the square footage feature, due to its larger values, might disproportionately influence the model, overshadowing the contribution of the number of bedrooms. As Goodfellow et al. (2016) discuss in their deep learning book, feature scaling can significantly improve the convergence speed and stability of gradient-based optimization algorithms.

Several techniques are commonly used for feature scaling and normalization. Standardization, also known as Z-score normalization, transforms features to have a mean of 0 and a standard deviation of 1. This is achieved by subtracting the mean of the feature from each value and then dividing by the standard deviation. Standardization is particularly useful when the data follows a roughly normal distribution. Consider the house price example: if the square footage feature is approximately normally distributed, standardization would transform it into a feature with a mean of 0 and a standard deviation of 1. Min-Max scaling, on the other hand, scales features to a specific range, typically between 0 and 1. This is done by subtracting the minimum value of the feature from each value and then dividing by the range[1] (the difference between the maximum and minimum values). Min-Max scaling is useful when you want to constrain the values of the features within a specific interval. A common question is when to use standardization versus Min-Max scaling. Standardization is generally preferred when the data follows a normal distribution or when the algorithm used is sensitive to the scale of the features (e.g., Support Vector Machines, K-Nearest Neighbors). Min-Max scaling might be more suitable when you have features with bounded ranges or when you want to preserve the original distribution of the data.

Another important aspect of feature scaling is handling outliers. Outliers can significantly affect the mean and standard deviation, leading to suboptimal scaling. Robust scaling techniques, such as using the median and interquartile range (IQR) instead of the mean and standard deviation, can mitigate the influence of outliers. For example, the RobustScaler in scikit-learn scales features using the median and IQR, making it less sensitive to outliers compared to the StandardScaler. Suppose your house price dataset contains a few extremely large houses that are outliers. Using robust scaling would prevent these outliers from unduly influencing the scaling of the other houses. A practical tip is to visualize the data after scaling to ensure that the scaling has been applied correctly and that there are no unexpected artifacts. Histograms or box plots can be used to check the distribution of the scaled features. Students often struggle with understanding the impact of feature scaling on different machine learning algorithms. Providing examples of how scaling affects the performance of algorithms like linear regression, logistic regression, and Support

Vector Machines can help them grasp the importance of this preprocessing step. Furthermore, emphasizing the need to apply the same scaling transformation to the test data as was applied to the training data is crucial for ensuring consistent results. By carefully choosing and applying appropriate feature scaling and normalization techniques, data scientists can improve the performance and robustness of their machine learning models.

Encoding Categorical Variables

Encoding categorical variables is a crucial step in preparing data for machine learning algorithms. Many algorithms, especially those based on mathematical formulations, require numerical input and cannot directly handle categorical data, which represents qualities or characteristics. Imagine you're building a model to predict customer churn for a telecom company. Features like "phone service type" (e.g., landline, mobile, none) or "internet service provider" (e.g., DSL, fiber optic, none) are categorical. These need to be transformed into numerical representations before they can be used in a model. As James et al. (2013) explain in their introduction to statistical learning, appropriate encoding of categorical variables is essential for model performance and interpretability.

Several techniques exist for encoding categorical variables. One-hot encoding is a widely used method that creates a new binary (0 or 1) column for each category. For the "phone service type" example, one-hot encoding would create three new columns: "phone_service_landline," "phone_service_mobile," and "phone_service_none." If a customer has mobile phone service, the "phone_service_mobile" column would have a value of 1, and the other two columns would have a value of 0. One-hot encoding is particularly suitable for nominal categorical variables, where there is no inherent order among the categories. Another common technique is label encoding, which assigns a unique integer to each category. For the "internet service provider" example, DSL might be encoded as 0, fiber optic as 1, and none as 2. Label encoding is suitable for ordinal categorical variables, where there is a meaningful order among the categories. However, it can also be used for nominal variables, but care must be taken to avoid implying an artificial order that doesn't exist. A common question is when to use one-hot encoding versus label encoding. One-hot encoding is generally preferred for nominal variables to avoid introducing spurious relationships between categories. Label encoding might be more appropriate for ordinal variables, as it preserves the order information.

Beyond one-hot and label encoding, other techniques exist for handling categorical variables, especially those with a large number of categories (high cardinality). Target encoding replaces each category with the mean of the target variable for that category. For example, if you're predicting customer churn, you might replace each internet service provider with the average churn rate for customers using that provider. Target encoding can be effective but is prone to overfitting if not used carefully. It's crucial to use techniques like cross-validation or regularization to mitigate overfitting when using target encoding. Another approach is to group less frequent categories into a single "other" category. This can reduce the dimensionality of the data and improve model performance, especially when dealing with high-cardinality categorical variables. Consider a dataset of cities: if there are many small cities with few data points, grouping them into an "other" category might be beneficial. Students often struggle with choosing the most appropriate encoding technique for a given situation. Providing them with examples of different types of categorical variables and discussing the trade-offs between different encoding methods can help them develop their judgment. Furthermore, emphasizing the importance of considering the specific machine learning algorithm being used and the potential impact of different encoding methods on model performance is crucial. By carefully encoding categorical variables, data scientists can effectively leverage all available information in their data and build more accurate and reliable predictive models.

Splitting Data into Training and Testing Sets

Splitting data into training and testing sets is a fundamental practice in machine learning, crucial for evaluating the performance of a model on unseen data and preventing overfitting. Imagine you're developing a model to predict customer preferences for new products. You wouldn't want to train and evaluate your model on the same data, as this could lead to overly optimistic performance estimates. The model might simply memorize the training data, performing well on it but failing to generalize to new, unseen customers. As Hastie et al. (2009) explain in their influential book on statistical learning, splitting data into training and testing sets allows us to simulate how the model will perform on real-world data.

The training set is used to train the machine learning model. The model learns the patterns and relationships in the training data, adjusting its parameters to minimize the prediction error. Think of it as the learning phase, where the model is exposed to the data and learns to make predictions. The testing set, on the other hand, is held back during training and used solely to evaluate the model's performance on unseen data. This provides an independent assessment of how well the model generalizes to new data. Using the customer preference example, the training set might consist of data from existing customers, while the testing set would contain data from a separate group of customers whose preferences are unknown to the model during training. A common question is how to determine the appropriate size of the training and testing sets. While there's no fixed rule, a common split is

80% for training and 20% for testing. However, this can vary depending on the size of the dataset. For smaller datasets, a larger proportion might be allocated to the training set to ensure the model has enough data to learn from.

Several techniques exist for splitting data. Simple random splitting randomly divides the data into training and testing sets. Stratified splitting ensures that the proportions of different classes or categories are preserved in both the training and testing sets. This is particularly important when dealing with imbalanced datasets, where some classes have significantly fewer examples than others. Consider a medical diagnosis dataset where the number of patients with a rare disease is much smaller than the number of patients without the disease.[1] Stratified splitting would ensure that both the training and testing sets have a representative proportion of patients with the rare disease. Another technique is time-based splitting, which is often used for time series data. In this case, the data is split chronologically, with earlier data used for training and later data used for testing. This simulates how the model will be used in practice, where it will be applied to future data. Students often struggle with understanding the importance of using a separate testing set and the potential pitfalls of evaluating a model on the training data. Providing clear examples of overfitting and explaining how a separate testing set helps detect overfitting is crucial. Furthermore, emphasizing the importance of keeping the testing set completely separate from the training process, including any preprocessing steps, is essential for ensuring a fair evaluation. By properly splitting data into training and testing sets, data scientists can obtain reliable estimates of model performance and avoid the pitfalls of overfitting, leading to more robust and generalizable models.

Part 2 Machine Learning Algorithms

Chapter 4 Introduction to Machine Learning

What is Machine Learning?

Machine learning (ML) is a subfield of artificial intelligence (AI) that focuses on enabling computers to learn from data without explicit programming. Instead of relying on hard-coded rules, ML algorithms identify patterns, make predictions, and improve their performance over time by being exposed to more data. Imagine you're developing a spam filter for email. Traditional programming would involve writing a complex set of rules to identify spam based on keywords, sender addresses, and other criteria. However, this approach is often brittle and difficult to maintain, as spammers constantly evolve their tactics. ML offers a more adaptive solution. By training an ML model on a large dataset of emails labeled as spam or not spam, the model can learn to identify spam patterns automatically, even if those patterns are not explicitly programmed. As Mitchell (1997) defines in his classic text, machine learning is concerned with the question of how to construct computer programs that automatically improve through experience.

At its core, ML involves building a model that can learn from data. This model can be a mathematical equation, a set of rules, or a more complex structure like a neural network. The training process involves feeding the model data and adjusting its parameters until it can accurately make predictions or classifications. In the spam filter example, the training data would consist of emails labeled as spam or not spam. The model would learn to identify features that are indicative of spam, such as the presence of certain keywords, suspicious sender addresses, or unusual email formatting. Once trained, the model can be used to classify new, unseen emails as spam or not spam. A key distinction between traditional programming and machine learning is that in ML, the focus is on learning the rules from data, rather than explicitly programming them. This makes ML particularly well-suited for tasks where the rules are complex, unknown, or constantly changing, such as spam filtering, image recognition, and natural language processing. A common question is how machine learning differs from statistics. While there's overlap, ML often emphasizes prediction and building systems that can perform tasks intelligently, while statistics often focuses on inference and understanding the underlying data generating process.

Machine learning has become increasingly prevalent in various aspects of our lives. From personalized recommendations on streaming services to self-driving cars, ML is powering many of the technologies we use every day. In the medical field, ML is being used to develop diagnostic tools, predict patient outcomes, and personalize treatment plans. In finance, ML is used for fraud detection, risk assessment, and algorithmic trading. The rapid advancement of ML has been fueled by the availability of large datasets, the development of powerful algorithms, and the increasing affordability of computing resources. As Jordan and Mitchell (2015) point out in their Science article, the field of machine learning is now experiencing a renaissance, driven by both theoretical advances and practical applications. Students often ask about the different types of machine learning. Introducing the three main categories – supervised learning, unsupervised learning, and reinforcement learning – with clear examples (e.g., supervised: image classification; unsupervised: customer segmentation; reinforcement: game playing) can help them grasp the fundamental concepts. Furthermore, discussing the ethical implications of ML, such as bias in algorithms or the potential impact on employment, is crucial for responsible development and deployment of ML systems.

Types of Machine Learning (Supervised, Unsupervised, Reinforcement)

Machine learning encompasses several distinct paradigms, each suited to different types of problems and data. The three primary categories are supervised learning, unsupervised learning, and reinforcement learning. Understanding the nuances of each type is crucial for selecting the appropriate approach for a given task. Imagine you're developing an AI-powered tutor. Supervised learning would be appropriate if you have a dataset of student exercises with correct answers. The algorithm learns to map exercises to correct answers, enabling it to grade new exercises. Unsupervised learning, on the other hand, would be useful if you want to group students based on their learning patterns without predefined categories. The algorithm would identify clusters of students with similar characteristics. Reinforcement learning could be used to personalize the learning experience, where the tutor learns to adapt its teaching strategies based on student performance and feedback. As Sutton and Barto (2018) explain in their comprehensive book on reinforcement learning, each learning paradigm addresses a unique set of challenges.

Supervised learning is the most common type of machine learning. It involves training a model on labeled data, where the input features and the corresponding target values are provided. The goal is to learn a mapping function that can accurately predict the target value for new, unseen input features. In the AI tutor example, the labeled data would consist of student exercises (input features) and their correct answers (target values). The supervised learning algorithm would learn to associate specific features of the exercises with the correct answers. Supervised learning algorithms can be used for various tasks, including classification (predicting a categorical target variable, e.g., spam or not spam) and regression (predicting a continuous target variable, e.g., house price). A common question is how to choose the right supervised learning algorithm for a given problem. The choice depends on several factors, including the type of data, the size of the dataset, and the desired performance metrics. Providing students with a range of examples and discussing the strengths and weaknesses of different algorithms (e.g., linear regression, logistic regression, decision trees) can help them make informed decisions.

Unsupervised learning deals with unlabeled data, where only the input features are provided. The goal is to discover patterns, structures, or relationships in the data without knowing the target values. In the AI tutor example, unsupervised learning could be used to group students based on their learning styles or to identify topics that students are struggling with. Common unsupervised learning tasks include clustering (grouping similar data points together, e.g., customer segmentation) and dimensionality reduction (reducing the number of features while preserving important information, e.g., principal component[1] analysis). A frequent question is how to evaluate the results of unsupervised learning algorithms, as there are no ground truth labels to compare against. Discussing internal validation metrics (e.g., silhouette score for clustering) and emphasizing the importance of domain expertise in interpreting the results can provide students with practical guidance.

Reinforcement learning is a different paradigm where an agent learns to interact with an environment by taking actions and receiving rewards or penalties. The goal is to learn a policy that maximizes the cumulative reward over time. In the AI tutor example, the reinforcement learning agent would learn to adapt its teaching strategies based on student performance and feedback, receiving rewards for effective teaching and penalties for ineffective teaching. Reinforcement learning is particularly well-suited for tasks that involve decision-making over time, such as game playing, robotics, and personalized recommendations. A common challenge for students is understanding the concept of delayed rewards and how the agent learns to associate actions with long-term consequences. Providing clear examples of reinforcement learning scenarios (e.g., a robot learning to navigate a maze) and explaining the concept of exploration and exploitation can help them grasp the fundamental concepts. By understanding the different types of machine learning, students can effectively choose the appropriate approach for a given problem and leverage the power of machine learning to solve real-world challenges.

Model Evaluation Metrics (Accuracy, Precision, Recall, F1-Score, RMSE, etc.)

Evaluating the performance of a machine learning model is crucial to understanding its effectiveness and ensuring its suitability for a given task. Choosing the right evaluation metric depends heavily on the specific problem and the type of model being used. Imagine you're developing a model to detect fraudulent credit card transactions. Simply measuring the overall accuracy might be misleading, as fraudulent transactions are typically much less frequent than legitimate transactions. A model that always predicts "legitimate" would have high accuracy but would be completely useless for fraud detection. As Provost and Kohavi (1998) discuss in their work on the foundations of machine learning, careful selection of evaluation metrics is essential for obtaining meaningful insights into model performance.

For classification problems, several metrics are commonly used. Accuracy measures the overall correctness of the model's predictions. However, as illustrated by the fraud detection example, accuracy can be misleading for imbalanced datasets. Precision measures the proportion of positive predictions that are actually correct. In the fraud detection scenario, precision would measure the proportion of transactions predicted as fraudulent that are truly fraudulent. Recall, on the other hand, measures the proportion of actual positive cases that are correctly predicted. In our example, recall would measure the proportion of all actual fraudulent transactions that are correctly identified by the model. The F1-score is the harmonic mean of precision and recall, providing a balanced measure of both. It's particularly useful when dealing with imbalanced datasets. A common question is when to prioritize precision versus recall. The answer depends on the specific application. If the cost of false positives is high (e.g., falsely flagging a legitimate transaction as fraudulent), precision should be prioritized. If the cost of false negatives is high (e.g., failing to detect a fraudulent transaction), recall should be prioritized. Often, there's a trade-off between precision and recall, and the F1-score helps balance these two metrics.

For regression problems, different evaluation metrics are used. Root Mean Squared Error (RMSE) is a commonly used metric that measures the average difference between the predicted and actual values. A lower RMSE indicates better model performance. Mean Absolute Error (MAE) is another metric that measures the average absolute difference between the predicted and actual values. Unlike RMSE, MAE is less sensitive to outliers. R-squared measures the proportion of variance in the target variable that is explained by the model. An R-squared value closer to 1 indicates better model fit. A frequent question is how to choose between RMSE and MAE. RMSE is more sensitive to outliers than MAE, so MAE might be preferred if the data contains outliers. RMSE is also differentiable, which makes it more convenient for optimization algorithms. Students often struggle with understanding the nuances of different evaluation metrics and how to interpret them. Providing clear examples and explaining the meaning of each metric in the context of specific problems can significantly improve their understanding. Furthermore, emphasizing the importance of considering the specific goals of the modeling task when choosing evaluation metrics is crucial for ensuring that the chosen metrics are aligned with the desired outcomes. By carefully selecting and interpreting appropriate evaluation metrics, data scientists can gain valuable insights into model performance and make informed decisions about model selection and deployment.

Chapter 5 Supervised Learning Algorithms

Linear Regression

Linear regression is a foundational supervised learning algorithm used for predicting a continuous target variable based on a linear relationship with one or more predictor variables. Imagine you're trying to predict house prices based on factors like square footage, number of bedrooms, and location. Linear regression assumes a linear relationship between these features and the house price. It finds the best-fitting line (or hyperplane in higher dimensions) that minimizes the difference between the predicted and actual prices. As Draper and Smith (1998) explain in their classic text on applied regression analysis, understanding the underlying theory and assumptions of linear regression is crucial for proper application and interpretation of results.

The theory behind linear regression involves finding the coefficients (weights) for each predictor variable that minimize a cost function. The most common cost function is the mean squared error (MSE), which measures the average squared difference between the predicted and actual values. Mathematically, the goal is to find the coefficients that minimize the sum of squared residuals. For simple linear regression with one predictor variable, the model can be represented as: $y = mx + b$, where y is the predicted value, x is the predictor variable, m is the slope, and b is the intercept. The process of finding the optimal m and b involves calculus and linear algebra, typically using techniques like ordinary least squares (OLS) regression. In multiple linear regression with multiple predictor variables, the model becomes: $y = \beta 0 + \beta 1x1 + \beta 2x2 + ... + \beta nxn$, where $\beta 0$ is the intercept and $\beta 1$, $\beta 2$, ..., βn are the coefficients for the predictor variables $x1$, $x2$, ..., xn, respectively. A common question is how linear regression handles non-linear relationships. While linear regression assumes linearity, it can be extended to model non-linear relationships by transforming the predictor variables (e.g., using polynomial features or logarithmic transformations).

Implementing linear regression with scikit-learn in Python is straightforward. First, you need to import the LinearRegression class from sklearn.linear_model. Then, you create an instance of the class and fit it to your training data using the fit() method, providing the predictor variables and the target variable as arguments. Once the model is trained, you can use the predict() method to make predictions on new, unseen data. Scikit-learn also provides methods to access the learned coefficients (using coef_) and the intercept (using intercept_). Consider the house price prediction example: you would load your data into a Pandas DataFrame, split it into training and testing sets, create a LinearRegression object, fit it to the training data, and then use it to predict house prices in the testing set. A practical tip is to evaluate the model's performance using appropriate metrics like RMSE or R-squared. Scikit-learn provides functions like mean_squared_error and r2_score for this purpose. Students often struggle with understanding the assumptions of linear regression, such as linearity, independence of errors, homoscedasticity, and normality of errors. Discussing these assumptions and their implications, perhaps referencing the work of Wooldridge (2016) on introductory econometrics, is crucial for responsible use of linear regression. Furthermore, emphasizing the importance of checking these assumptions using diagnostic plots and statistical tests can prevent misinterpretations and ensure the validity of the results.

Logistic Regression

Logistic regression, despite its name, is a classification algorithm used for predicting the probability of a categorical outcome. It's particularly useful when the target variable has two possible outcomes (binary classification), such as predicting whether a customer will click on an advertisement (click/no click) or diagnosing a disease (positive/negative). Imagine you're building a model to predict customer churn for a subscription service. Logistic regression can estimate the probability that a customer will cancel their subscription based on factors like usage patterns, demographics, and customer service interactions. As Hosmer and Lemeshow (2000) detail in their book on applied logistic regression, it provides a statistically sound framework for binary classification problems.

The theory behind logistic regression involves modeling the probability of the outcome using a sigmoid function. The sigmoid function transforms a linear combination of the predictor variables into a probability between 0 and 1. Mathematically, the model can be represented as: $p = 1 / (1 + \exp(-z))$, where p is the probability of the positive outcome, z is a linear combination of the predictor variables ($z = \beta_0 + \beta_1 x_1 + \beta_2 x_2 + \dots + \beta_n x_n$), and $\exp()$ is the exponential function. The goal is to find the coefficients (β_0, β_1, ..., β_n) that maximize the likelihood of observing the actual outcomes in the training data. This is typically done using maximum likelihood estimation (MLE). A common question is how logistic regression handles multi-class classification problems (more than two outcomes). While the basic logistic regression is for binary classification, it can be extended to multi-class problems using techniques like one-vs-rest (where a separate logistic regression model is trained for each class) or multinomial logistic regression (which directly models the probabilities of all classes).

Implementing logistic regression with scikit-learn is straightforward. First, import the LogisticRegression class from sklearn.linear_model. Create an instance of the class and fit it to your training data using the fit() method, providing the predictor variables and the target variable as arguments. Once the model is trained, use the predict() method to predict the class labels for new data and the predict_proba() method to get the predicted probabilities. Scikit-learn also provides options to specify regularization techniques (L1 or L2) to prevent overfitting. Consider the customer churn prediction example: you would load your data, preprocess it as needed (e.g., encoding categorical variables), split it into training and testing sets, create a LogisticRegression object, fit it to the training data, and then use it to predict churn probabilities for customers in the testing set. A practical tip is to evaluate the model's performance using metrics like accuracy, precision, recall, F1-score, and AUC-ROC. Scikit-learn provides functions like accuracy_score, precision_score, recall_score, f1_score, and roc_auc_score for this purpose. Students often struggle with understanding the interpretation of the coefficients in logistic regression. Explaining that the coefficients represent the change in the log-odds of the outcome for a one-unit change in the predictor variable, perhaps referencing the work of Agresti (2015) on categorical data analysis, can help clarify this concept. Furthermore, emphasizing the importance of checking model assumptions, such as linearity of the logit and independence of errors, is crucial for ensuring the validity of the results.

Decision Trees

Decision trees are a versatile supervised learning algorithm used for both classification and regression tasks. They work by recursively partitioning the data space into smaller and smaller regions based on the values of the features. Imagine you're building a model to predict whether a customer will purchase a specific product online. A decision tree might first split the data based on the customer's age, then further split each age group based on their browsing history, and so on, until it reaches a leaf node that predicts the purchase decision. As Breiman et al. (1984) introduced in their seminal work on classification and regression trees, decision trees offer an intuitive and interpretable way to model complex relationships in data.

The theory behind decision trees involves selecting the best feature to split the data at each node. This selection is based on criteria like information gain (for classification) or variance reduction (for regression). Information gain measures the reduction in entropy achieved by splitting the data on a particular feature. Entropy is a measure of the impurity or disorder of a set of data points. For regression tasks, variance reduction measures the decrease in the variance of the target variable achieved by the split. The process of building the tree involves recursively selecting the best split until a stopping criterion is met, such as reaching a maximum depth or a minimum number of samples in a leaf node. A common question is how decision trees handle categorical features. Decision trees can handle categorical features directly by creating branches for each category. For numerical features, the tree typically finds a threshold value to split the data into two groups.

Implementing decision trees with scikit-learn is straightforward. For classification, import the DecisionTreeClassifier class from sklearn.tree. For regression, import the DecisionTreeRegressor class. Create an instance of the chosen class and fit it to your training data using the fit() method. Once the model is trained, use the predict() method to make predictions on new data. Scikit-learn also provides methods to visualize the learned tree structure, which can be very helpful for understanding how the model makes decisions. Consider the product purchase prediction example: you would load your data, preprocess it as needed (e.g., encoding categorical variables), split it into training and testing sets, create a DecisionTreeClassifier object, fit it to the training data, and then use it to predict purchase decisions for customers in the testing set. A practical tip is to tune the hyperparameters of the decision tree, such as the maximum depth or the minimum number of samples in a leaf node, to prevent overfitting. Scikit-learn provides tools like GridSearchCV or RandomizedSearchCV for this purpose. Students often struggle with understanding the concept of overfitting in decision trees. Explaining how complex trees can memorize the training data and fail to generalize to new data, and demonstrating the effect of pruning or limiting tree depth on overfitting, is crucial. Furthermore, discussing the advantages and disadvantages of decision trees, such as their interpretability, ability to handle both categorical and numerical data, and susceptibility to overfitting, is essential for informed model selection. By understanding the theory and implementation of decision trees, data scientists can effectively leverage this versatile algorithm for a wide range of machine learning tasks.

Random Forest

Random Forest is an ensemble learning method that combines multiple decision trees to improve prediction accuracy and robustness. Imagine you're building a model to predict the risk of a patient developing a certain disease. A single decision tree might be susceptible to overfitting or sensitive to small changes in the training data. A Random Forest, on the other hand, creates a multitude of decision trees, each trained on a random subset of the data and a random subset of the features. The final prediction is then[1] made by aggregating the predictions of all the individual trees, typically through voting for classification or averaging for regression. As Breiman (2001) introduced in his seminal paper, Random Forests offer a powerful and versatile approach to improve the performance and stability of decision tree models.

The theory behind Random Forests builds upon the concept of decision trees. However, instead of training a single tree on the entire dataset, Random Forests create multiple trees, each trained on a bootstrapped sample (randomly sampled with replacement) of the data. This introduces diversity among the trees, as they are exposed to slightly different versions of the training data. Furthermore, at each node of a tree, the best feature to split on is chosen from a random subset of features, rather than considering all available features. This further increases the diversity and reduces the correlation between the trees. The final prediction is made by aggregating the predictions of all the trees. For classification, this is typically done through majority voting, where the class with the most votes from the individual trees is chosen as the final prediction. For regression, the predictions of the trees are averaged to obtain the final prediction. A common question is why Random Forests are less prone to overfitting than individual decision trees. The answer lies in the combination of bootstrapping and feature subsampling. Bootstrapping creates multiple training sets, each slightly different, which reduces the variance of the model. Feature subsampling further decorrelates the trees, making them less likely to make the same errors.

Implementing Random Forests with scikit-learn is straightforward. For classification, import the RandomForestClassifier class from sklearn.ensemble. For regression, import the RandomForestRegressor class. Create an instance of the chosen class and fit it to your training data using the fit() method. You can specify the number of trees to create using the n_estimators parameter. Once the model is trained, use the predict() method to make predictions on new data. Consider the disease risk prediction example: you would load your data, preprocess it as needed, split it into training and testing sets, create a RandomForestClassifier object, fit it to the training data, and then use it to predict the risk of disease for patients in the testing set. A practical tip is to tune the hyperparameters of the Random Forest, such as the number of trees, the maximum depth of the trees, or the minimum number of samples in a leaf node, to further improve performance. Scikit-learn provides tools like GridSearchCV or RandomizedSearchCV for this purpose. Students often ask about the interpretability of Random Forests, given that they consist of multiple trees. While individual trees can be visualized, interpreting an entire Random Forest can be challenging. However, feature importance can be assessed by measuring how often each feature is used for splitting

71

across all trees. Discussing the trade-offs between interpretability and predictive accuracy, and emphasizing the importance of understanding the limitations of complex models, is crucial for responsible use of Random Forests. By understanding the theory and implementation of Random Forests, data scientists can effectively leverage this powerful ensemble method for a wide range of machine learning tasks.

Support Vector Machines (SVM)

Support Vector Machines (SVMs) are powerful supervised learning algorithms used for both classification and regression tasks. They are particularly effective in high-dimensional spaces and when dealing with complex datasets. Imagine you're building a model to classify images of cats and dogs. SVMs aim to find the optimal hyperplane that maximally separates the data points of the two classes. As Cortes and Vapnik (1995) introduced in their seminal paper, SVMs offer a robust and theoretically sound approach to classification and regression.

The theory behind SVMs involves finding the hyperplane that maximizes the margin, which is the distance between the hyperplane and the nearest data points (support vectors).[1] Maximizing the margin improves the generalization ability of the model, reducing the risk of overfitting. For linearly separable data, the optimal hyperplane can be found analytically. However, real-world data is often not linearly separable. In such cases, SVMs use the kernel trick to map the data into a higher-dimensional space where it becomes linearly separable. The kernel trick allows SVMs to operate in the high-dimensional space without explicitly computing the coordinates of the data points in that space, which can be computationally expensive. Common kernel functions include linear, polynomial, and radial basis function (RBF) kernels. Mathematically, SVMs involve solving an optimization problem to find the optimal hyperplane. This typically involves using techniques like quadratic programming. A common question is how SVMs handle non-linearly separable data. The kernel trick is the key to handling such data. By mapping the data to a higher-dimensional space,

SVMs can find a separating hyperplane even when the data is not linearly separable in the original space.

Implementing SVMs with scikit-learn is straightforward. For classification, import the SVC class from sklearn.svm. For regression, import the SVR class. Create an instance of the chosen class and fit it to your training data using the fit() method. You can specify the kernel function using the kernel parameter. For example, kernel='rbf' uses the RBF kernel. Once the model is trained, use the predict() method to make predictions on new data. Consider the cat vs. dog image classification example: you would load your image data, extract relevant features (e.g., using convolutional neural networks), split the data into training and testing sets, create an SVC object, fit it to the training data, and then use it to classify images in the testing set. A practical tip is to tune the hyperparameters of the SVM, such as the kernel parameters (e.g., gamma for the RBF kernel) and the regularization parameter C, to optimize performance. Scikit-learn provides tools like GridSearchCV or RandomizedSearchCV for this purpose. Students often struggle with understanding the concept of the kernel trick. Explaining how it allows SVMs to operate in high-dimensional spaces without explicitly computing the coordinates, perhaps using visual analogies, can help clarify this concept. Furthermore, discussing the advantages and disadvantages of SVMs, such as their effectiveness in high-dimensional spaces, ability to model complex relationships, and computational cost for large datasets, is essential for informed model selection. By understanding the theory and implementation of SVMs, data scientists can effectively leverage this powerful algorithm for a wide range of machine learning tasks.

K-Nearest Neighbors (KNN)

K-Nearest Neighbors (KNN) is a simple yet powerful supervised learning algorithm used for both classification and regression.[1] It classifies a new data point based on the majority class among its k-nearest neighbors in the training data. Imagine you're building a recommendation system for movies. KNN could recommend movies to a user based on the movies watched by users with similar taste profiles. As Cover and Hart (1967) introduced in their early work, KNN is a non-parametric algorithm that makes no assumptions about the underlying data distribution, making it flexible for various datasets.

The theory behind KNN is straightforward. Given a new data point, the algorithm calculates the distance between it and all the data points in the training set. Then, it selects the k-nearest neighbors based on the chosen distance metric (e.g., Euclidean distance, Manhattan distance). For classification, the algorithm assigns the new data point to the class that is most frequent among its k-nearest neighbors. For regression,[2] the algorithm predicts the average (or median) value of the target variable for its k-nearest neighbors. The choice of k is a crucial hyperparameter that affects the performance of the algorithm. A small k can make the model sensitive to noise in the data, while a large k can smooth out the decision boundaries but might also include irrelevant neighbors. A common question is how to choose the optimal value of k. Techniques like cross-validation can be used to evaluate the performance of the model for different values of k and select the one that generalizes best to unseen data.

Implementing KNN with scikit-learn is easy. For classification, import the KNeighborsClassifier class from sklearn.neighbors. For regression, import the KNeighborsRegressor class. Create an instance of the chosen class and fit it to your training data using the fit() method. You can specify the value of k using the n_neighbors parameter. Once the model is trained, use the predict() method to make predictions on new data. Consider the movie recommendation example: you would load your user-movie rating data, preprocess it as needed, split it into training and testing sets, create a KNeighborsClassifier or KNeighborsRegressor object, fit it to the training data, and then use it to recommend movies to users in the testing set. A practical tip is to scale the features before applying KNN, as the distance calculation is sensitive to the scale of the features. Scikit-learn provides tools like StandardScaler or MinMaxScaler for this purpose. Students often struggle with understanding the computational cost of KNN, especially for large datasets. Explaining that the algorithm needs to calculate the distance between the new data point and all the training data points, and discussing techniques like KD-trees or ball trees to speed up the search for nearest neighbors, is crucial. Furthermore, discussing the advantages and disadvantages of KNN, such as its simplicity, ability to handle both classification and regression, and sensitivity to feature scaling and irrelevant features, is essential for informed model selection. By understanding the theory and implementation of KNN, data scientists can effectively leverage this versatile algorithm for a wide range of machine learning tasks, particularly when the data distribution is unknown or complex.

Chapter 6 Unsupervised Learning Algorithms

K-Means Clustering

K-means clustering is a popular unsupervised learning algorithm used to partition data points into k distinct clusters based on their similarity. Imagine you're a marketing analyst trying to segment customers based on their purchasing behavior. K-means clustering can group customers with similar purchase patterns together, allowing you to tailor marketing campaigns to each segment. As MacQueen (1967) introduced in his early work, k-means is a relatively simple yet effective algorithm for clustering.

The theory behind k-means involves iteratively assigning data points to the nearest cluster center (centroid) and then updating the centroids based on the mean of the data points assigned to each cluster. The algorithm starts by randomly initializing k centroids. Then, it assigns each data point to the nearest centroid based on a chosen distance metric (e.g., Euclidean distance). After all data points are assigned, the algorithm recalculates the centroids as the mean of the data points assigned to each cluster. These two steps (assignment and update) are repeated until the centroids no longer change significantly or a maximum number of iterations is reached. The goal is to minimize the within-cluster sum of squares (WCSS), which measures the sum of the squared distances between each data point and its assigned centroid. A common question is how to choose the optimal value of k. The elbow method is a popular technique for this purpose. It involves running the k-means algorithm for different values of k and plotting the WCSS against k. The "elbow" point in the plot, where the rate of decrease in WCSS starts to slow down, is often considered the optimal k. Another technique is the silhouette score, which measures how similar a data point is to its own cluster compared to other clusters.

Implementing k-means clustering with scikit-learn is straightforward. Import the KMeans class from sklearn.cluster. Create an instance of the class, specifying the number of clusters k using the n_clusters parameter. Fit the model to your data using the fit() method. Once the model is trained, use the predict() method to assign data points to clusters. You can also access the cluster centers using the cluster_centers_ attribute. Consider the customer segmentation example: you would load your customer data, preprocess it as needed, create a KMeans object, fit it to the data, and then use it to segment customers into different groups. A practical tip is to scale the features before applying k-means, as the distance calculation is sensitive to the scale of the features. Scikit-learn provides tools like StandardScaler or MinMaxScaler for this purpose. Students often struggle with understanding the limitations of k-means, such as its sensitivity to the initial centroid initialization and its assumption of spherical clusters. Explaining that k-means can get stuck in local optima and might not perform well on non-convex or irregularly shaped clusters, and discussing alternative clustering algorithms like DBSCAN or hierarchical clustering for such cases, is crucial. Furthermore, emphasizing the importance of interpreting the resulting clusters in the context of the problem domain is essential for deriving meaningful insights from the clustering results. By understanding the theory and implementation of k-means, data scientists can effectively leverage this widely used algorithm for a variety of unsupervised learning tasks, particularly when seeking to identify groups or patterns in data.

Naive Bayes

Naive Bayes is a probabilistic classifier based on Bayes' theorem, with a "naive" assumption of feature independence. Despite its simplicity, it often performs surprisingly well in real-world applications, particularly in text classification and spam filtering. Imagine you're building a spam filter for email. Naive Bayes could learn the probability of certain words appearing in spam emails and use these probabilities to classify new emails as spam or not spam. As Rennie et al. (2003) discuss in their work on text classification with naive Bayes, its efficiency and effectiveness make it a popular choice for such tasks.

The theory behind Naive Bayes involves calculating the posterior probability of a class given the observed features. Bayes' theorem provides a way to calculate this posterior probability based on the prior probabilities of the classes and the likelihood of the features given each class. The "naive" assumption is that the features are independent of each other, given the class. This assumption simplifies the calculation of the likelihood, making the algorithm computationally efficient. Mathematically, the posterior probability of class C given features $F1$, $F2$, ..., Fn can be calculated as: $P(C|F1, F2, ..., Fn) = [P(F1|C) * P(F2|C) * ... * P(Fn|C) * P(C)] / P(F1, F2, ..., Fn)$. The naive assumption allows us to multiply the individual likelihoods $P(Fi|C)$ together. In practice, we often work with the log of the probabilities to avoid numerical underflow. A common question is how Naive Bayes handles continuous features. While the basic Naive Bayes assumes discrete features, it can be adapted to handle continuous features by assuming a specific distribution for each feature, such as a Gaussian distribution.

Implementing Naive Bayes with scikit-learn is straightforward. For discrete features (e.g., word counts in text classification), use the MultinomialNB class from sklearn.naive_bayes. For continuous features, use the GaussianNB class. Create an instance of the chosen class and fit it to your training data using the fit() method. Once the model is trained, use the predict() method to make predictions on new data. Consider the spam filter example: you would load your email data, preprocess it (e.g., converting emails to numerical feature vectors representing word counts), split it into training and testing sets, create a MultinomialNB object, fit it to the training data, and then use it to classify new emails in the testing set. A practical tip is to use techniques like TF-IDF (Term Frequency-Inverse Document Frequency) to weight the word counts in text classification, which can improve performance. Students often struggle with understanding the naive assumption and its implications. Explaining that while the assumption is often violated in real-world data, Naive Bayes can still perform well due to its simplicity and ability to handle high-dimensional data, is crucial. Furthermore, discussing the advantages and disadvantages of Naive Bayes, such as its efficiency, ease of implementation, and sensitivity to feature independence and zero probabilities, is essential for informed model selection. By understanding the theory and implementation of Naive Bayes, data scientists can effectively leverage this simple yet powerful algorithm for various tasks, particularly in text classification and other applications where the naive assumption is reasonable or the data is high-dimensional.

Chapter 7 Neural Networks

Introduction to Neural Networks

Neural networks, inspired by the structure and function of the human brain, are a powerful class of machine learning algorithms capable of learning complex patterns and representations from data. They are composed of interconnected nodes, or neurons, organized in layers. Imagine you're building a system to recognize handwritten digits. A neural network could take the pixel values of an image as input and, through a series of interconnected layers, learn to identify the digit represented in the image. As Rumelhart et al. (1986) described in their groundbreaking work, the backpropagation algorithm enabled the training of multi-layered neural networks, unlocking their potential for complex tasks.

The basic unit of a neural network is the neuron. Each neuron receives input from other neurons or from the input data, performs a simple mathematical operation (typically a weighted sum of the inputs followed by an activation function), and passes the output to other neurons in the network. The activation function introduces non-linearity, which is crucial for the network to learn complex patterns. Common activation functions include sigmoid, ReLU (Rectified Linear Unit), and tanh (hyperbolic tangent). Neurons are organized in layers: an input layer, one or more hidden layers, and an output layer. The input layer receives the raw data, the hidden layers process the data and extract features, and the output layer produces the final predictions. A common question is why neural networks need hidden layers. Hidden layers allow the network to learn hierarchical representations of the data. For example, in image recognition, the first hidden layer might learn to detect edges, the second hidden layer might learn to combine edges into shapes, and the third hidden layer might learn to combine shapes into objects.

Neural networks learn by adjusting the weights of the connections between neurons. This is typically done through a process called backpropagation, which involves calculating the error between the network's predictions and the actual target values, and then using this error to update the weights in a way that reduces the error. The training process involves iteratively feeding the network data, calculating the error, and updating the weights until the network's performance on the training data reaches a satisfactory level. A crucial aspect of neural networks is the choice of architecture, which includes the number of layers, the number of neurons in each layer, and the type of activation functions. This choice often depends on the specific problem and requires experimentation. A frequent question is how to choose the right architecture for a given problem. While there are some general guidelines, it often involves trial and error, and techniques like cross-validation can be used to evaluate the performance of different architectures. Furthermore, understanding the challenges of training neural networks, such as vanishing gradients and overfitting, and techniques to address these challenges, such as regularization and dropout, is crucial for building effective neural network models. By understanding the fundamental concepts of neural networks, including their structure, function, and training process, students can begin to explore this powerful class of algorithms and their applications in a wide range of fields.

Basics of Deep Learning

Deep learning is a subfield of machine learning that focuses on neural networks with multiple layers (often many layers, hence "deep"). These deep neural networks have proven remarkably effective at solving complex problems in areas like image recognition, natural language processing, and speech recognition. Imagine building a system to translate spoken language in real-time. Deep learning models, trained on vast amounts of audio and text data, can learn the intricate relationships between sounds, words, and meanings, enabling accurate and fluent translations. As LeCun et al. (2015) highlight in their influential review, deep learning has revolutionized many areas of artificial intelligence.

The "depth" in deep learning refers to the multiple layers of interconnected neurons in the network. Each layer learns to extract increasingly abstract and hierarchical features from the input data. For example, in image recognition, the first layers might detect simple features like edges and corners, while deeper layers learn to combine these features into more complex shapes and objects. This hierarchical feature learning allows deep learning models to capture intricate patterns in the data that shallower networks struggle with. A key characteristic of deep learning is its ability to learn these features automatically from raw data, reducing the need for manual feature engineering. This is a significant advantage, especially for complex data like images and text, where designing effective features can be challenging. A common question is how deep learning differs from traditional machine learning. While both involve learning from data, deep learning emphasizes the use of deep neural networks with multiple layers, enabling automatic feature extraction and handling of complex data. Traditional machine learning often relies on manually engineered features and simpler models.

Several types of deep neural networks are commonly used, each suited to different types of data and tasks. Convolutional Neural Networks (CNNs) are particularly effective for image and video data, leveraging the concept of convolutions to detect spatial hierarchies of features. Recurrent Neural Networks (RNNs) are designed for sequential data, such as text and time series, using feedback loops to capture temporal dependencies. For example, LSTMs (Long Short-Term Memory networks), a type of RNN, are often used in natural language processing tasks like machine translation. Autoencoders are used for unsupervised learning tasks, such as dimensionality reduction and feature extraction, by learning to reconstruct the input data. A frequent question is how to choose the right type of deep neural network for a given problem. The choice depends on the type of data (images, text, time series) and the specific task (classification, regression, generation). Providing students with examples of different network architectures and their applications can help them make informed decisions. Furthermore, understanding the challenges of training deep learning models, such as the need for large amounts of data and computational resources, and techniques to address these challenges, such as transfer learning and distributed training, is crucial for building effective deep learning systems. By understanding the basics of deep learning, including its key concepts, different network architectures, and training considerations, students can begin to explore this rapidly evolving field and its potential to solve a wide range of real-world problems.

Building a Simple Neural Network with TensorFlow/Keras

Building a simple neural network with TensorFlow/Keras is a fundamental skill for anyone venturing into deep learning. TensorFlow is a powerful open-source library for numerical computation and large-scale machine learning, while Keras provides a user-friendly API for building and training neural networks on top of TensorFlow (and other backends). Imagine you're building a model to classify handwritten digits from the MNIST dataset. This is a classic introductory problem in deep learning, and TensorFlow/Keras makes it relatively easy to implement a solution. As Abadi et al. (2016) detail in their TensorFlow documentation, understanding the fundamental building blocks of neural networks and how to implement them with TensorFlow/Keras is crucial for tackling more complex deep learning tasks.

The process of building a neural network with TensorFlow/Keras typically involves several steps. First, you need to define the architecture of the network. This includes specifying the number of layers, the type of each layer (e.g., dense, convolutional, recurrent), the number of neurons in each layer, and the activation functions. For the MNIST digit classification, a simple architecture might consist of an input layer, one or two hidden layers with ReLU activation, and an output layer with softmax activation. The input layer would receive the pixel values of the image, the hidden layers would learn to extract features, and the output layer would produce the probabilities for each digit (0-9). Keras provides a sequential API that makes it easy to define this architecture layer by layer. A common question is how to choose the appropriate architecture. While there are some general guidelines, it often involves experimentation and depends on the specific problem and dataset. Starting with a simple architecture and gradually increasing complexity is a good approach.

Once the architecture is defined, you need to compile the model. This involves specifying the optimizer, the loss function, and the metrics you want to track during training. The optimizer is the algorithm used to update the weights of the network during training (e.g., Adam, SGD). The loss function measures the error between the network's predictions and the actual target values (e.g., categorical cross-entropy for multi-class classification). The metrics are used to evaluate the performance of the model (e.g., accuracy). For the MNIST example, you might use the Adam optimizer, categorical cross-entropy loss, and accuracy as the metric. Keras provides a compile() method for this purpose. A frequent question is how to choose the right optimizer and loss function. The choice depends on the specific problem and the type of output. Providing students with a range of examples and explaining the characteristics of different optimizers and loss functions can help them make informed decisions.

After compiling the model, you need to train it on your data. This involves feeding the training data to the model and adjusting the weights using the optimizer and loss function. Keras provides a fit() method for this purpose. You can specify the number of epochs (iterations over the entire training data) and the batch size (number of samples processed at each step). For the MNIST example, you would load the MNIST dataset, preprocess it (e.g., normalizing pixel values), split it into training and testing sets, and then train the model using the fit() method. Finally, you can evaluate the trained model on the testing set to assess its performance on unseen data. Keras provides an evaluate() method for this purpose. Students often struggle with understanding the concept of epochs and batch size. Explaining their impact on training time and model performance, and discussing techniques like early stopping to prevent overfitting, is crucial. By following these steps, students can build and train simple neural networks using TensorFlow/Keras and gain a solid foundation for exploring more advanced deep learning techniques.

Training and Evaluating Neural Networks

Training and evaluating neural networks are crucial steps in the deep learning workflow. The training process involves feeding data to the network and adjusting its weights to minimize the prediction error. Evaluation, on the other hand, assesses the performance of the trained network on unseen data to ensure its generalization ability. Imagine you're training a neural network to recognize different types of flowers. The training process involves showing the network images of flowers labeled with their species and adjusting the network's weights until it can accurately classify the flowers. Evaluation involves testing the network on a separate set of flower images to see how well it performs on unseen examples. As Goodfellow et al. (2016) explain in their deep learning book, a robust training and evaluation process is essential for building effective neural network models.

The training process typically involves several key steps. First, the data is preprocessed, which might include normalizing pixel values for images, tokenizing text for natural language processing, or scaling numerical features. Then, the data is split into training, validation, and testing sets. The training set is used to train the network, the validation set is used to monitor the network's performance during training and tune hyperparameters, and the testing set is used for the final evaluation. The network is then trained by feeding it data in batches and updating the weights using an optimization algorithm (e.g., Adam, SGD). The loss function, which measures the error between the network's predictions and the actual target values, guides the weight updates. A common question is why we need a separate validation set.

The validation set helps prevent overfitting, where the network memorizes the training data and performs poorly on unseen data. By monitoring the network's performance on the validation set, we can tune hyperparameters and stop training early if the performance starts to degrade.

During training, several metrics are typically tracked, such as accuracy, precision, recall, F1-score for classification tasks, and mean squared error or R-squared for regression tasks. These metrics provide insights into the network's performance and help identify potential issues. For example, if the training accuracy is high but the validation accuracy is low, it might indicate overfitting. A frequent question is how to choose the right metrics for a given task. The choice depends on the specific problem and the desired outcomes. For example, in medical diagnosis, recall might be more important than precision, as it's crucial to identify all positive cases, even if it means some false positives.

After training, the network is evaluated on the testing set to assess its generalization ability. This provides an unbiased estimate of how well the network will perform on new, unseen data. The same metrics used during training are typically used for evaluation. It's crucial to keep the testing set completely separate from the training process, including any preprocessing steps, to ensure a fair evaluation. Students often struggle with understanding the concept of overfitting and how to prevent it. Explaining how monitoring the validation performance and using techniques like regularization, dropout, or early stopping can help mitigate overfitting is crucial. Furthermore, discussing the importance of interpreting the evaluation results in the context of the problem domain and considering the limitations of the model is essential for responsible use of neural networks. By understanding the training and evaluation process, including data preprocessing, hyperparameter tuning, metric selection, and overfitting prevention, students can effectively build and deploy neural network models for a wide range of applications.

Part 3 Web Development with Flask

Chapter 8 Introduction to Flask

What is Flask?

Flask is a microframework for web development in Python. It's designed to be lightweight and flexible, giving developers control over the core components of their web applications while providing tools and features for common tasks. Unlike larger, more monolithic frameworks, Flask doesn't impose a specific project structure or a large set of pre-built functionalities. This makes it an excellent choice for smaller projects, APIs, and situations where you need fine-grained control or want to integrate with other libraries. Imagine you're building a simple web application to display data from a machine learning model. Flask's lightweight nature allows you to quickly create the web interface without the overhead of a larger framework. As Grinberg (2018) explains in his book on Flask web development, its simplicity and extensibility make it a popular choice for both beginners and experienced developers.

Flask's "micro" nature means it focuses on providing the essentials: routing (mapping URLs to functions), request handling, and templating. Routing allows you to define different URLs that your application will respond to. For example, you could define a route /predict that handles requests to your machine learning model. Request handling involves processing incoming requests from users, such as form submissions or API calls. Flask provides tools for accessing request data, such as form values or JSON payloads. Templating allows you to generate dynamic HTML pages by embedding Python code within HTML templates. This makes it easy to create web pages that display data from your application. A common question is why choose Flask over other web frameworks like Django. While Django is a powerful and feature-rich framework, it can be overkill for smaller projects. Flask's lightweight nature makes it easier to learn and faster to develop simple web applications. However, for larger, more complex projects, Django's built-in features and project structure might be more advantageous.

Flask is often used in conjunction with other libraries to build complete web applications. For example, you might use a database library like SQLAlchemy to interact with a database, a form library like WTForms to handle form submissions, or a machine learning library like scikit-learn to integrate machine learning models. Flask's extensibility allows you to choose the libraries that best suit your needs. Consider the machine learning model web application example: you could use scikit-learn to train your model, Flask to create the web interface, and a library like requests to send data to the model for prediction. A frequent question is how Flask compares to other microframeworks like Bottle or Pyramid. While these frameworks share some similarities, Flask's large and active community, extensive documentation, and wide range of extensions make it a popular choice. Flask's flexibility also makes it well-suited for building RESTful APIs, which are commonly used to connect web applications to backend services or machine learning models. By understanding the core concepts of Flask, including routing, request handling, and templating, and its integration with other libraries, students can begin building their own web applications and deploying their machine learning models to the web.

Setting Up Flask

Setting up Flask involves a few straightforward steps to get your development environment ready for building web applications. This process typically involves installing Python, setting up a virtual environment, installing Flask, and creating a basic Flask application. A well-structured setup is crucial for managing dependencies and ensuring that your projects are isolated from each other. Imagine you're starting a new web project that relies on specific versions of libraries. A virtual environment allows you to install these specific versions without affecting other Python projects on your system. As Miguel Grinberg emphasizes in his Flask Mega-Tutorial, establishing a clean development environment is a best practice for web development.

The first step is to ensure you have Python installed. Flask requires Python 3.7 or higher. You can download the latest version of Python from the official Python website (python.org). Once Python is installed, it's highly recommended to create a virtual environment. This is a self-contained directory that contains its own Python installation and packages, allowing you to manage dependencies on a per-project basis. You can create a virtual environment using the venv module (included with Python 3). Open your terminal or command prompt, navigate to your project directory, and run the command python3 -m venv venv. This will create a virtual environment named "venv" (you can choose any name). A common question is why virtual environments are so important. They prevent conflicts between different project dependencies and ensure that your projects are reproducible. Without virtual environments, installing a package for one project might unintentionally break another project that relies on a different version of the same package.

After creating the virtual environment, you need to activate it. On Windows, you can activate it by running venv\Scripts\activate. On macOS and Linux, you can activate it by running source venv/bin/activate. Once the virtual environment is activated, you'll see the name of the environment (e.g., "venv") in your terminal prompt. Now you can install Flask. You can do this using pip, the Python package installer. Run the command pip install Flask to install the latest version of Flask. A frequent question is how to manage dependencies for a Flask project. Creating a requirements.txt file is a best practice. This file lists all the packages your project depends on. You can create this file by running pip freeze > requirements.txt. Later, you can install the dependencies listed in this file by running pip install -r requirements.txt.

Finally, you can create a basic Flask application. Create a new Python file (e.g., app.py) and add the following code:

```Python
from flask import Flask

app = Flask(__name__)

@app.route("/")
def hello():
    return "Hello, World!"

if __name__ == "__main__":
```

```
app.run(debug=True)
```

This code creates a Flask application object, defines a route for the root URL ("/"), and starts the development server. You can run this application by running python app.py in your terminal. Then, you can open your web browser and navigate to http://127.0.0.1:5000/ to see the "Hello, World!" message. Students often struggle with understanding the purpose of the __name__ == "__main__" block. Explaining that it ensures the app.run() function is only called when the script is run directly, and not when it's imported as a module, can clarify this concept. By following these steps, students can set up their development environment for Flask and start building web applications.

Flask Basics (Routing, Templates, Static Files)

Flask's core functionality revolves around routing, templating, and serving static files. These three elements are fundamental for creating dynamic and interactive web applications. Routing maps URLs to specific functions that handle requests. Templating allows you to generate dynamic HTML pages by embedding Python code within HTML files. Serving static files enables you to include images, CSS stylesheets, and JavaScript files in your web application. Imagine you're building a web application to display data visualizations generated by a machine learning model. Routing would determine which function handles the request to display a specific visualization. Templating would allow you to create the HTML page that embeds the visualization. Serving static files would allow you to include CSS stylesheets to style the page and JavaScript files to add interactivity. As Grinberg (2018) explains, mastering these basics is essential for building robust and maintainable Flask applications.

Routing in Flask is achieved using the @app.route() decorator. This decorator associates a URL pattern with a specific function. For example, @app.route("/about") would map the URL /about to the function defined immediately below the decorator. Inside the function, you can process the request and return a response, which can be a string, an HTML document, or a redirect. Flask also supports dynamic routes, where parts of the URL are variable. For example, @app.route("/user/<username>") would capture the username from the URL and pass it as an argument to the associated function. A common question is how to handle different HTTP methods (GET, POST, PUT, DELETE) for the same URL. Flask allows you to specify the HTTP methods that a route should handle using the methods argument in the @app.route() decorator. For example, @app.route("/submit", methods=["GET", "POST"]) would handle both GET and POST requests to the /submit URL.

Templating in Flask is typically done using Jinja2, a powerful templating engine. Templates are HTML files that can contain placeholders for dynamic content. You can pass data from your Flask functions to the templates, which will then be rendered into HTML. Jinja2 provides a variety of control structures, such as loops and conditional statements, that allow you to generate dynamic HTML. For example, you could use a loop to iterate over a list of data and display each item in a table. Flask provides the render_template() function to render templates. You pass the name of the template file and any data you want to pass to the template as arguments. A frequent question is how to organize templates in a Flask project. A common practice is to create a templates directory in your project and store all your template files in this directory.

Serving static files in Flask is done by placing them in a static directory in your project.

Flask automatically serves files from this directory. You can include static files in your templates using the url_for() function. For example, <img src="{{ url_for('static', filename='images/logo.png') }}"> would include the image logo.png from the static/images directory. A common question is how to structure the static directory. It's a good practice to organize static files into subdirectories based on their type (e.g., css, js, images). This makes it easier to manage your static files. By understanding routing, templating, and serving static files, students can create dynamic and interactive web applications using Flask. They can build web interfaces that handle user requests, display data, and include styling and interactivity through static files.

Chapter 9 Integrating Data Science with Flask

Loading CSV Datasets in Flask

Integrating data science workflows with web applications often requires the ability to load and process data within the web framework itself. Flask, being a flexible microframework, allows for seamless integration with data science libraries like Pandas, making it straightforward to load and manipulate CSV datasets directly within your web application. Imagine you're building a web dashboard to visualize sales data. You might have the sales data stored in a CSV file, and you need to load this data into your Flask application to generate charts and tables. As Grinberg (2018) demonstrates, Flask's integration with Python's data science ecosystem enables efficient data handling within web contexts.

The primary way to load CSV datasets in Flask is by leveraging the Pandas library. Pandas provides the read_csv() function, which can efficiently parse CSV files and load the data into a DataFrame, a powerful data structure for manipulation and analysis. Within your Flask application, you can import Pandas and then use read_csv() to load the data. For example, you might have a route in your Flask application that handles requests to display sales data. Inside this route function, you would call pd.read_csv('sales_data.csv') to load the data. A crucial consideration is where to store the CSV file. A common practice is to store it in a directory accessible to your Flask application, such as a "data" directory within your project. You can then specify the relative path to the file when calling read_csv(). A common question is how to handle potential errors when loading the CSV file, such as the file not existing or being corrupted. Using try-except blocks is essential for robust error handling. You can wrap the read_csv() call in a try block and handle potential FileNotFoundError or pd.errors.ParserError exceptions in the except block, perhaps displaying an error message to the user.

Once the data is loaded into a Pandas DataFrame, you can perform various data manipulation and analysis tasks within your Flask application. For example, you might filter the data, calculate aggregates, or create new features. Pandas provides a rich set of functionalities for these tasks. Consider the sales data example: you might filter the data by region, calculate the total sales for each product, or create a new column representing the profit margin. A practical tip is to load the data only once when the Flask application starts, rather than loading it every time a request is made. This can significantly improve performance, especially for large datasets. You can load the data into a global variable or store it in a cache when the application starts and then access it within your route functions. Students often struggle with understanding how to pass the data from the Flask application to the HTML templates for display. Using Jinja2 templating, you can pass the Pandas DataFrame or its processed data to the template and then use Jinja2's templating constructs to render the data in HTML tables or charts. By integrating Pandas with Flask, data scientists can easily create web interfaces to display and interact with their data, enabling them to share their insights and models with a wider audience.

Building APIs for Machine Learning Models

Building APIs for machine learning models is a crucial step in deploying these models for real-world use. A well-defined API allows other applications or services to easily interact with your model, sending data and receiving predictions. Flask, with its lightweight nature and ease of use, is an ideal framework for creating such APIs. Imagine you've trained a model to predict customer churn. Building an API with Flask would allow other parts of your company's system, like the customer relationship management (CRM) platform, to send customer data to your model and receive churn predictions in real-time. As Grinberg (2018) illustrates, Flask's simplicity makes it efficient for creating API endpoints.

The core of building an API with Flask involves defining routes that handle specific requests and return responses in a structured format, typically JSON. You would define a route that accepts data as input (e.g., via a POST request) and then processes this data using your machine learning model. The model's prediction is then formatted as a JSON response and sent back to the client. Consider the customer churn prediction example: you might define a route /predict_churn that accepts customer data (e.g., usage patterns, demographics) in JSON format. Inside this route function, you would load the JSON data, preprocess it as needed, pass it to your trained machine learning model for prediction, and then return the prediction (e.g., churn probability) as a JSON response. A critical consideration is how to serialize and deserialize data, especially when dealing with complex data structures. The jsonify() function in Flask is helpful for converting Python dictionaries to JSON responses. For handling more complex data, you might consider using libraries like marshmallow or pydantic for schema validation and serialization. A common question is how to handle different data types in the API request. Clearly defining the expected data types in the API documentation and validating the input data within the Flask route is essential for robust API design.

Once the API endpoint is defined, you need to load your trained machine learning model. A best practice is to load the model only once when the Flask application starts, rather than loading it every time a request is made. This can significantly improve performance, especially for large models. You can load the model into a global variable or store it in a cache when the application starts and then access it within your route functions. A frequent question is how to handle errors within the API. Using try-except blocks is essential for robust error handling. You can wrap the model prediction call in a try block and handle potential exceptions in the except block, returning appropriate error messages as JSON responses. For example, you might return a 500 Internal Server Error if the model encounters an unexpected error. Another important consideration is API documentation. Clearly documenting the API endpoints, the expected input data format, and the format of the responses is crucial for other developers to use your API effectively. Tools like Swagger or OpenAPI can be used to generate interactive API documentation. By building APIs for your machine learning models using Flask, you can make these models accessible to other applications and services, enabling their integration into real-world systems and workflows. Students often struggle with understanding how to structure the API request and response. Providing clear examples of JSON payloads and explaining how to handle them within the Flask route using request.get_json() can significantly improve their understanding. Furthermore, emphasizing the importance of security considerations, such as authentication and authorization, when building APIs is crucial for responsible API development.

Creating Dynamic Web Pages with Flask Templates

Creating dynamic web pages with Flask templates is a fundamental aspect of integrating data science results into a user-friendly web interface. Flask's templating engine, Jinja2, allows you to embed Python code within HTML files, enabling you to generate web pages that dynamically display data, visualizations, and other content. Imagine you've built a machine learning model that predicts house prices. You can use Flask templates to create a web page where users can input house features, and the predicted price is displayed dynamically on the page. As Grinberg (2018) explains, Jinja2's powerful features make it an ideal tool for creating dynamic web content in Flask applications.

The process of creating dynamic web pages with Flask templates involves several key steps. First, you need to create your HTML templates. These are HTML files that contain placeholders for dynamic content, typically enclosed in double curly braces {{ ... }}. These placeholders can represent variables, expressions, or control structures. For example, {{ house_price }} would display the value of the house_price variable passed from your Flask application. Jinja2 also provides control structures like {% for item in items %} to iterate over a list of items and {% if condition %} to conditionally display content. Consider the house price prediction example: you could create a template that includes input fields for house features and a placeholder for the predicted price. A common question is how to pass data from the Flask application to the templates. You can pass data to the templates using the render_template() function in Flask. This function takes the name of the template file and any variables you want to pass to the template as keyword arguments.

Once you have your templates, you need to render them from your Flask routes. Inside your route functions, you can use the render_template() function to generate the HTML output. This function takes the name of the template file and any data you want to pass to the template as arguments. Flask will then process the template, replacing the placeholders with the actual values, and return the resulting HTML to the user's browser. For the house price prediction example, you would have a route that handles the user's input, passes the input data to your machine learning model for prediction, and then renders the template, passing the predicted price as a variable. A frequent question is how to organize templates in a Flask project. A best practice is to create a "templates" directory in your project and store all your template files in this directory. Flask will automatically look for templates in this directory.

Beyond simple variable substitution, Jinja2 allows you to use filters to format data. For example, {{ house_price | round(2) }} would display the house_price rounded to two decimal places. Jinja2 also supports template inheritance, allowing you to create a base template with common elements and then extend it in other templates. This promotes code reuse and makes it easier to maintain your templates. Students often struggle with understanding how to use control structures in Jinja2. Providing clear examples of loops and conditional statements, and demonstrating how to use them to generate dynamic HTML, can significantly improve their understanding. Furthermore, emphasizing the importance of separating presentation logic (in the templates) from application logic (in the Flask routes) is crucial for building maintainable web applications. By mastering Flask templates, data scientists can create interactive web interfaces to showcase their data science work, making their models and insights accessible to a broader audience.

Chapter 10 Building a Data-Driven Web Application

Designing the Application Structure

Designing the application structure is a crucial first step in building a data-driven web application with Flask. A well-structured application is easier to maintain, scale, and understand, especially as the project grows in complexity. Think of building a web application that not only displays data visualizations but also allows users to interact with the data, perhaps filtering it or requesting specific analyses. A clear structure will help organize the code for data loading, processing, model integration, and web presentation. As Grinberg (2018) advises, a well-defined structure promotes maintainability and collaboration.

A common approach for structuring Flask applications is to use a modular design, separating different functionalities into distinct modules or blueprints. This allows for better organization and code reusability. For example, you could have a blueprint for handling data loading and preprocessing, another for integrating your machine learning models, and a third for defining the web routes and templates. Within each module, you should further organize your code into functions and classes that perform specific tasks. Consider the data visualization application: you might have a module for loading data from various sources (CSV, database, etc.), a module for generating the visualizations using libraries like Matplotlib or Plotly, and a module for defining the Flask routes that connect the data and visualizations to the web interface. A question that often arises is how to choose the right level of modularity. While separating functionalities into distinct modules is generally a good idea, it's essential to avoid over-engineering the application structure. A balance should be struck between modularity and simplicity, keeping the structure manageable and understandable.

Another important aspect of application structure is how you manage static files (CSS, JavaScript, images) and templates. As discussed previously, a common practice is to have a "static" directory for static files and a "templates" directory for HTML templates. Within these directories, you can further organize files into subdirectories based on their type (e.g., "static/css", "static/js", "templates/data_vis"). This makes it easier to manage and locate these files. Consider the data visualization application again: you might have CSS files for styling the web pages, JavaScript files for adding interactivity, and image files for logos or icons. Organizing these files into subdirectories ensures a clean and organized project structure. A frequent question is how to handle database interactions. If your application interacts with a database, it's a good idea to create a separate module or blueprint for database operations. This module would contain functions for connecting to the database, querying data, and updating data. This separation of concerns makes it easier to manage database interactions and keeps the web routes focused on handling user requests.

Finally, consider how you will handle configuration. It's often a good practice to separate configuration settings from the application code.

You can use environment variables, configuration files, or a combination of both to manage settings like database credentials, API keys, or debugging flags. This makes it easier to deploy the application in different environments (development, testing, production) without modifying the code. Students often struggle with understanding how to connect the different modules or blueprints together. Providing clear examples of how to import functions and classes from one module into another, and how to register blueprints with the Flask application, is crucial. Furthermore, emphasizing the importance of documenting the application structure and the purpose of each module is essential for maintainability and collaboration. By carefully designing the application structure, data scientists can build robust and scalable web applications that effectively integrate data science workflows with user-friendly web interfaces.

Integrating Machine Learning Models into Flask

Integrating machine learning models into a Flask web application is the core of deploying your data science work to a wider audience. It allows users to interact with your trained models through a web interface, sending data and receiving predictions in real-time. Imagine you've developed a model to predict customer churn. Integrating it into Flask allows your company's sales or marketing teams to use this model through a simple web interface to identify at-risk customers. As Grinberg (2018) explains, Flask's flexibility makes it suitable for integrating various machine learning workflows.

The process typically involves several key steps. First, you need to load your trained machine learning model. This is best done once when the Flask application starts, rather than every time a prediction is requested, to improve efficiency. You can achieve this by loading the model into a global variable or using a caching mechanism. Consider the customer churn prediction example: you might have saved your trained model using pickle or joblib. You would load this model when the Flask app initializes and store it in a variable, say churn_model. A common question is how to handle different model file formats. Libraries like pickle, joblib, and specialized model serialization tools for specific frameworks (e.g., TensorFlow SavedModel) can be used to load models depending on how they were saved. It's crucial to ensure compatibility between the environment where the model was trained and the Flask deployment environment.

Next, you need to create a Flask route that handles prediction requests. This route will receive data from the user (e.g., through a form or API call), preprocess it as needed, pass it to your loaded machine learning model for prediction, and then return the prediction to the user. For the churn prediction example, the route might receive customer data (age, usage, etc.) from a form. You would then preprocess this data (e.g., scaling, encoding), pass it to churn_model.predict(), and return the churn probability to the user. A crucial consideration is how to handle different data types and formats received from the user. Input validation and data type conversion are essential to prevent errors. Flask's request object provides access to form data, JSON payloads, and other request data, but it's important to validate this data before passing it to the model.

Finally, you need to format the model's output and present it to the user. This might involve displaying the prediction directly, visualizing it using charts or graphs, or storing it in a database. Flask's templating engine, Jinja2, can be used to generate dynamic HTML pages that display the model's output. Consider the churn prediction example again: you might display the churn probability in a user-friendly format on the web page. A frequent question is how to handle batch predictions. For scenarios where you need to make predictions on multiple data points at once, you can modify the Flask route to accept a batch of data, iterate over it, make predictions for each data point, and return the predictions as a list or JSON array. Students often struggle with understanding how to preprocess the input data in the same way it was preprocessed during model training. Maintaining consistency in preprocessing steps is essential. One approach is to save the preprocessing steps (e.g., scaling parameters, encoding mappings) along with the trained model and load them as well. By carefully integrating machine learning models into Flask, data scientists can create interactive web applications that allow users to benefit from their trained models, making their work impactful and accessible.

Displaying Results on the Web Interface

Displaying results on a web interface is the final step in making your data-driven Flask application user-friendly and informative. It's not enough to have a working machine learning model or data analysis pipeline; the results must be presented in a way that is easily understood and actionable by the end-user. Imagine you've built a web application that recommends personalized music playlists. The recommendations themselves are useless unless they are displayed clearly on the web page, perhaps with album art, song titles, and links to listen to the music. As Grinberg (2018) demonstrates, Flask's integration with templating engines makes it straightforward to create visually appealing and informative web interfaces.

The primary way to display results in a Flask application is by using templates. Templates are HTML files that contain placeholders for dynamic content. You can pass data from your Flask routes to the templates, and the templating engine (Jinja2 by default) will replace the placeholders with the actual data when the page is rendered. Consider the music playlist recommendation example: you might have a template that displays a list of recommended songs. You would pass the list of songs (perhaps as a Python list of dictionaries, where each dictionary represents a song) from your Flask route to the template. Within the template, you would use Jinja2's looping constructs ({% for song in songs %}) to iterate over the list and display each song's information (title, artist, album art) in a visually appealing format. A common question is how to display different types of results, such as tables, charts, or maps. For tabular data, you can use HTML tables directly within your templates or consider using JavaScript libraries like DataTables for more interactive tables. For charts and graphs, you can use Python libraries like Matplotlib, Plotly, or Bokeh to generate the visualizations and then embed them in your templates. For maps, you can use libraries like Folium or integrate with mapping services like Google Maps or Leaflet. The choice depends on the complexity and interactivity you require.

Beyond simply displaying data, consider how to present the information clearly and effectively. Use appropriate formatting, styling, and layout to make the results easy to understand. For example, use headings, labels, and clear visual hierarchy to organize the content. Consider using CSS frameworks like Bootstrap to quickly create a responsive and visually appealing layout. For the music playlist example, you might use album art as visual cues, display song titles and artists in a clear font, and provide links to listen to the songs. A frequent question is how to handle large amounts of data. For very large datasets, loading all the data at once and passing it to the template might be inefficient. Consider using techniques like pagination or lazy loading to load and display data in chunks. You could also use JavaScript to fetch data from the server asynchronously as the user interacts with the page.

Finally, interactivity can greatly enhance the user experience. Consider adding features like sorting, filtering, searching, or drill-down capabilities to allow users to explore the data. JavaScript libraries can be very helpful for adding interactivity to your web pages. For the music playlist example, you might allow users to sort the playlist by artist or genre, or to filter the playlist based on their mood. Students often struggle with integrating JavaScript libraries into their Flask applications. Providing clear examples of how to include JavaScript files in your templates and how to use JavaScript to interact with the data passed from Flask can significantly improve their understanding. Furthermore, emphasizing the importance of user experience design principles when displaying results is crucial for creating effective and user-friendly web applications. By carefully considering how to display results, data scientists can make their work accessible and impactful, enabling users to gain valuable insights from their data and models.

Handling User Input and Forms

Handling user input and forms is a critical aspect of building interactive and data-driven web applications with Flask. Forms provide a way for users to submit data to your application, which can then be processed and used for various purposes, such as making predictions with a machine learning model, updating a database, or triggering specific actions. Imagine you're building a web application that allows users to submit feedback on a product. Forms would be used to collect the feedback, which could then be stored in a database or analyzed to identify areas for improvement. As Grinberg (2018) explains, Flask's integration with form handling libraries makes it straightforward to process user input.

The process of handling user input and forms in Flask typically involves several steps. First, you need to create your HTML form. This involves defining the form elements, such as text fields, checkboxes, radio buttons, and submit buttons, and specifying the method (usually POST) and action attributes of the form. The method attribute determines how the form data is sent to the server (POST is generally preferred for form submissions), and the action attribute specifies the URL that handles the form submission. Consider the product feedback example: you might have a form with a text area for the feedback and a submit button. A common question is how to handle different form element types. Flask provides access to the submitted form data through the request.form object, which is a dictionary-like object containing the values of the form elements. You can access the value of a specific element using its name. For example, if the text area for feedback is named "feedback", you can access its value using request.form['feedback'].

Next, you need to create a Flask route that handles the form submission. This route will be associated with the action URL specified in the form. Inside the route function, you can access the submitted form data using the request.form object. You can then process this data as needed. For the product feedback example, the route would receive the feedback text, store it in a database, and perhaps display a thank you message to the user. A crucial consideration is how to validate the user input. It's essential to validate the submitted data to prevent errors and ensure data integrity. You can use libraries like WTForms or validate the data manually within your route function. For example, you might check if required fields are filled, if the data is in the correct format, or if it meets certain criteria.

Finally, you need to provide feedback to the user after the form is submitted. This might involve displaying a success message, redirecting the user to another page, or displaying error messages if the form submission failed. Flask's templating engine, Jinja2, can be used to generate dynamic HTML pages that display this feedback. Consider the product feedback example again: after the feedback is submitted, you might redirect the user to a thank you page. A frequent question is how to handle file uploads. Flask provides access to uploaded files through the request.files object. You can save the uploaded files to the server's file system or process them in memory. It's crucial to validate the uploaded files to ensure they are of the correct type and size. Students often struggle with understanding how to handle form submissions and data validation. Providing clear examples of how to access form data, validate it, and provide feedback to the user can significantly improve their understanding. Furthermore, emphasizing the importance of security considerations, such as preventing cross-site scripting (XSS) attacks, when handling user input is crucial for responsible web development. By carefully handling user input and forms, data scientists can create interactive web applications that allow users to easily interact with their data and models.

Part 4 Advanced Topics and Deployment

Chapter 11 Model Optimization and Tuning

Hyperparameter Tuning (Grid Search, Random Search)

Hyperparameter tuning is a critical step in optimizing the performance of machine learning models. Unlike model parameters, which are learned during training, hyperparameters are settings that control the learning process itself. These can include things like the learning rate, the depth of a decision tree, or the regularization strength. Finding the optimal combination of hyperparameters can significantly impact a model's accuracy and generalization ability. Imagine you're training a deep learning model for image classification. The number of layers, the number of neurons in each layer, the learning rate, and the batch size are all hyperparameters that need to be tuned to achieve the best performance. As Bergstra et al. (2011) demonstrate, effective hyperparameter tuning can lead to substantial improvements in model performance.

Two common approaches for hyperparameter tuning are grid search and random search. Grid search involves creating a grid of all possible combinations of hyperparameter values within a specified range. The model is then trained and evaluated for each combination, and the combination that yields the best performance is selected. Consider the image classification example: you might define a grid of values for the learning rate (e.g., 0.001, 0.01, 0.1) and the batch size (e.g., 32, 64, 128). Grid search would then train and evaluate the model for all nine possible combinations of these hyperparameters. While grid search is guaranteed to find the optimal combination within the specified range, it can be computationally expensive, especially when dealing with many hyperparameters or large datasets. A common question is how to define the range of hyperparameter values to search. Domain knowledge and prior experience can be helpful in defining reasonable ranges. It's also a good practice to start with a broader range and then refine it based on the results of the initial search.

Random search, on the other hand, involves randomly sampling hyperparameter combinations from a specified distribution. Instead of evaluating all possible combinations, random search explores a random subset of the hyperparameter space. This can be more efficient than grid search, especially when some hyperparameters are more important than others. Consider the image classification example again: you might define a distribution for the learning rate (e.g., a logarithmic distribution) and a distribution for the batch size (e.g., a uniform distribution). Random search would then randomly sample values for these hyperparameters from the defined distributions and train and evaluate the model for each sampled combination. A frequent question is when to use grid search versus random search. Grid search is generally preferred when the number of hyperparameters is small and the computational cost is not a major concern. Random search is more suitable for high-dimensional hyperparameter spaces or when the computational cost is a limiting factor.

Scikit-learn provides tools like GridSearchCV and RandomizedSearchCV to implement grid search and random search, respectively. These tools automate the process of training and evaluating the model for different hyperparameter combinations. You simply need to define the model, the hyperparameter grid or distributions, and the evaluation metric, and the tools will handle the rest. Students often struggle with understanding the concept of cross-validation, which is often used in conjunction with hyperparameter tuning. Explaining how cross-validation helps to estimate the model's performance on unseen data and prevents overfitting is crucial. Furthermore, discussing the importance of choosing an appropriate evaluation metric for hyperparameter tuning, and how it should align with the goals of the modeling task, is essential for effective model optimization. By understanding and applying hyperparameter tuning techniques, data scientists can significantly improve the performance and generalization ability of their machine learning models.

Cross-Validation Techniques

Cross-validation is a crucial technique in machine learning for evaluating model performance and ensuring its generalizability to unseen data. It addresses the problem of overfitting, where a model performs well on the training data but poorly on new data. Imagine you're developing a model to predict customer churn. If you train and evaluate your model on the same data, it might overfit and give you an overly optimistic estimate of its performance. Cross-validation provides a more robust way to assess how well your model will perform in the real world. As Kohavi (1995) explains in his work on cross-validation, it provides a more reliable estimate of model performance than simply splitting the data into a single training and testing set.

The basic idea behind cross-validation is to partition the data into multiple folds, or subsets. The model is then trained and evaluated multiple times, each time using a different fold as the testing set and the remaining folds as the training set. The performance metrics from each evaluation are then averaged to give an overall estimate of the model's performance. K-fold cross-validation is a common technique where the data is divided into k folds. For each iteration, one fold is used as the testing set, and the other $k-1$ folds are used as the training set. For example, in 5-fold cross-validation, the data is divided into five folds. The model is trained five times, each time using a different fold as the testing set and the other four folds as the training set. The performance metrics from the five evaluations are then averaged to give an overall estimate of the model's performance. A common question is how to choose the value of k. While there's no fixed rule, a common choice is *k=5* or *k=10*. Larger values of *k* generally provide a more reliable estimate of performance but also increase the computational cost.

Stratified k-fold cross-validation is a variation of k-fold cross-validation that is particularly useful when dealing with imbalanced datasets, where some classes have significantly fewer examples than others.[1] Stratified k-fold ensures that the proportion of each class is roughly the same in each fold. This is important to prevent some folds from having a disproportionate number of examples from a particular class, which could bias the evaluation. Consider a medical diagnosis dataset where the number of patients with a rare disease is much smaller than the number of patients without the disease.[2] Stratified k-fold would ensure that each fold has a representative proportion of patients with the rare disease. A frequent question is how cross-validation differs from using a single train-test split. While a single train-test split is simpler, it can be sensitive to the specific data points that are chosen for the training and testing sets. Cross-validation provides a more robust estimate of performance by averaging over multiple train-test splits.

Scikit-learn provides tools like KFold, StratifiedKFold, and cross_val_score to implement cross-validation. These tools simplify the process of partitioning the data, training and evaluating the model multiple times, and aggregating the results. Students often struggle with understanding the concept of bias-variance tradeoff in the context of cross-validation. Explaining how cross-validation helps to find a balance between bias and variance, and how it can be used to select the best model among several candidates, is crucial. Furthermore, discussing the computational cost of cross-validation and the importance of choosing an appropriate cross-validation strategy based on the size of the dataset and the available resources is essential for practical model evaluation. By understanding and applying cross-validation techniques, data scientists can obtain more reliable estimates of model performance and build models that generalize well to unseen data.

Handling Overfitting and Underfitting

Overfitting and underfitting are two common challenges in machine learning that can significantly impact the performance of a model. Overfitting occurs when a model learns the training data too well, including noise and irrelevant details, leading to poor generalization to new, unseen data. Underfitting, on the other hand, occurs when a model is too simple to capture the underlying patterns in the data, resulting in poor performance[1] on both the training and testing[2] data. Imagine you're building a model to predict house prices. An overfit model might memorize specific details of the training houses, like the exact number of windows or the names of the previous owners, and fail to accurately predict the prices of new houses. An underfit model might simply predict the average house price, ignoring important features like square footage or location. As Hastie et al. (2009) explain in their book on statistical learning, understanding and addressing overfitting and underfitting is crucial for building effective machine learning models.

Several techniques can be used to combat overfitting. Regularization is a common approach that adds a penalty to the loss function, discouraging the model from learning overly complex patterns. L1 regularization encourages sparsity in the model's weights, effectively performing feature selection. L2 regularization, also known as ridge regression, shrinks the weights towards zero, reducing the model's complexity. Another technique is data augmentation, which involves creating new training examples by applying transformations to existing examples, such as rotating or flipping images. This increases the diversity of the training data and helps the model generalize better. Pruning, which is often used for decision trees, involves simplifying the tree by removing branches that contribute little to the model's accuracy. Dropout, which is commonly used in neural networks, randomly deactivates neurons during training, forcing the network to learn more robust features. A common question is how to choose between L1 and L2 regularization. L1 regularization is useful when you suspect that only a few features are relevant, as it can effectively perform feature selection. L2 regularization is generally a good choice when you want to prevent overfitting without necessarily performing feature selection.

Underfitting, on the other hand, can be addressed by increasing the model's complexity. This might involve using a more complex model, such as a higher-degree polynomial regression or a deeper neural network, or adding more features to the data. Feature engineering, which involves creating new features from existing ones, can also help address underfitting. For example, in the house price prediction example, you might create a new feature that represents the interaction between square footage and location. A frequent question is how to determine whether a model is overfitting or underfitting. Comparing the model's performance on the training and validation sets is crucial. If the model performs well on the training set but poorly on the validation set, it's likely overfitting. If the model performs poorly on both the training and validation sets, it's likely underfitting.

Scikit-learn provides tools for implementing regularization, such as RidgeClassifier and LassoClassifier for L2 and L1 regularization, respectively. TensorFlow and Keras provide mechanisms for implementing dropout and other regularization techniques in neural networks. Students often struggle with understanding the bias-variance tradeoff in the context of overfitting and underfitting. Explaining how increasing model complexity reduces bias but increases variance, and how regularization helps to find a balance between bias and variance, is crucial. Furthermore, discussing the importance of using cross-validation to evaluate model performance and detect overfitting and underfitting is essential for building robust and generalizable models. By understanding and applying these techniques, data scientists can effectively address overfitting and underfitting and build machine learning models that perform well on unseen data.

Chapter 12 Deploying the Flask Application

Introduction to Deployment

Deploying a Flask application makes it accessible to users over the internet or within a network. It transforms a local development project into a live, functional web application. Imagine you've built a Flask app that predicts plant health based on images. Deployment is the process of putting that application on a server so that anyone can access it through their web browser and use it to assess their plants. As Grinberg (2018) explains, deployment involves several key considerations, from choosing the right hosting environment to ensuring the application's scalability and security.

The deployment process typically involves choosing a hosting environment. Several options exist, each with its own pros and cons. Platform as a Service (PaaS) providers, like Heroku or PythonAnywhere, offer a simplified deployment experience, handling server management and scaling automatically. This is a good option for smaller projects or when you want to focus on development rather than infrastructure. Infrastructure as a Service (IaaS) providers, like AWS EC2 or Google Compute Engine, give you more control over the server environment but require more technical expertise. This is a good option for larger, more complex applications or when you need specific server configurations. Another option is to deploy to a virtual private server (VPS), which gives you a balance of control and ease of use. A common question is how to choose the right hosting environment. The choice depends on several factors, including the size and complexity of the application, the expected traffic, the budget, and the technical expertise of the development team.

Once you've chosen a hosting environment, you need to prepare your application for deployment. This might involve installing necessary dependencies, configuring environment variables, and setting up a production-ready web server. For example, you might need to install Gunicorn or uWSGI, which are production-grade WSGI servers commonly used with Flask. You'll also need to configure your web server to handle static files (CSS, JavaScript, images) efficiently. A frequent question is how to manage dependencies during deployment. Using a requirements.txt file to list all the project's dependencies is essential. You can then install these dependencies on the server using pip install -r requirements.txt. It's also a good practice to use a version control system like Git to manage your code and make deployment easier.

The actual deployment process varies depending on the chosen hosting environment. PaaS providers often offer simple deployment tools, such as Git integration or command-line interfaces. IaaS providers require more manual setup, including configuring the server, installing the necessary software, and deploying the application code. Regardless of the chosen method, it's crucial to test the deployed application thoroughly to ensure it's working as expected. Students often struggle with understanding the difference between a development server (like the one started with app.run()) and a production-ready web server. Explaining that the development server is not suitable for production use due to security and performance reasons is crucial. Furthermore, discussing the importance of security considerations, such as using HTTPS and protecting against common web vulnerabilities, is essential for responsible deployment. By understanding the deployment process, including choosing the right hosting environment, preparing the application, and deploying the code, students can make their Flask applications accessible to the world.

Deploying Flask Apps on Heroku

Deploying Flask applications on Heroku offers a streamlined and relatively straightforward path to making your web applications accessible online. Heroku, a Platform as a Service (PaaS), handles much of the server infrastructure and management, allowing developers to focus primarily on the application code itself. Imagine you've built a Flask application that analyzes and visualizes data from social media. Deploying it on Heroku allows you to share this application with a wider audience without needing to manage servers or deal with complex infrastructure configurations. As Heroku's documentation explains, their platform simplifies the deployment process for various web application frameworks, including Flask.

The process of deploying a Flask application on Heroku involves several key steps. First, you need to create a Heroku account if you don't already have one. Then, you need to install the Heroku Command Line Interface (CLI), which allows you to interact with Heroku from your terminal. The CLI provides commands for creating Heroku apps, pushing code, and managing your deployed applications. After installing the CLI, you need to log in to your Heroku account using the heroku login command. A common question is why a CLI is necessary. The CLI provides a convenient and programmatic way to manage your Heroku applications, making it easier to automate deployments and manage multiple applications.

Next, you need to prepare your Flask application for deployment. This typically involves creating a Procfile and a requirements.txt file. The

Procfile tells Heroku how to run your application. For a Flask application, the Procfile typically contains a line like web: gunicorn app:app, where app:app refers to your Flask application instance. Gunicorn is a production-grade WSGI HTTP server commonly used with Flask. The requirements.txt file lists all the Python packages your application depends on. You can create this file by running pip freeze > requirements.txt. Heroku uses this file to install the necessary packages on their servers. A frequent question is why a Procfile is needed. Heroku needs to know how to start your application. The Procfile provides this information, specifying the command to run when your application is deployed.

Finally, you can deploy your application to Heroku. This typically involves creating a Git repository for your project, adding your application code and the Procfile and requirements.txt files to the repository, and then pushing the repository to Heroku. Heroku will then automatically build your application, install the dependencies, and start the web server. You can create a Heroku app using the heroku create command and then push your code using git push heroku main (assuming "main" is your main branch). After the deployment is complete, you can open your application in your web browser using the heroku open command. Students often struggle with understanding the role of Git in the deployment process. Explaining that Git is used to track changes to the application code and that Heroku uses Git to receive and deploy the code can clarify this concept. Furthermore, discussing the importance of configuring environment variables on Heroku for sensitive information, such as database credentials or API keys, is crucial for secure deployments. By following these steps, students can easily deploy their Flask applications on Heroku and make them accessible to the world.

Deploying Flask Apps on AWS or Google Cloud

Deploying Flask applications on cloud platforms like AWS (Amazon Web Services) or Google Cloud Platform (GCP) offers greater control and scalability compared to simpler platforms like Heroku. These platforms provide a comprehensive suite of services, allowing you to customize your deployment environment, manage infrastructure, and scale your application as needed. Imagine you've built a complex Flask application that uses machine learning models, interacts with a database, and handles a high volume of traffic. Deploying it on AWS or GCP allows you to configure the server environment precisely, optimize performance, and automatically scale resources based on demand. As the documentation for both AWS and GCP emphasizes, these platforms provide robust and scalable solutions for deploying web applications.

Deploying on AWS or GCP typically involves several key steps. First, you need to create an account with the chosen cloud provider and familiarize yourself with their console or command-line interface. Both platforms offer a variety of services, and understanding the relevant services for web application deployment (e.g., EC2 for AWS, Compute Engine for GCP, and load balancing services) is essential. A common question is how to choose between AWS and GCP. The choice often depends on factors like familiarity with the platform, pricing, specific service offerings, and integration with other tools. Both platforms offer free tiers for initial experimentation, allowing you to explore their services before committing to paid plans.

Next, you need to set up a virtual machine (VM) instance. This VM will host your Flask application. You'll need to choose the operating system, instance type (which determines the resources allocated to the VM), and storage options. For a Flask application, a Linux-based VM is typically used. You'll also need to configure security groups (for AWS) or firewall rules (for GCP) to allow traffic to your application's port (usually port 80 or 443 for HTTP/HTTPS). A crucial consideration is security. Properly configuring security groups or firewall rules is essential to protect your application from unauthorized access. You should also ensure that your VM is running a secure operating system and that all software is up to date.

After setting up the VM, you need to connect to it (usually via SSH) and install the necessary software, including Python, pip, your application's dependencies (using pip install -r requirements.txt), and a production-ready WSGI server like Gunicorn or uWSGI. You'll also need to configure your web server (e.g., Nginx or Apache) to act as a reverse proxy, forwarding requests to your Flask application running on Gunicorn or uWSGI. A frequent question is why a reverse proxy is needed. A reverse proxy provides several benefits, including load balancing, caching, and security. It sits in front of your Flask application and handles incoming requests, improving performance and security.

Finally, you need to deploy your application code to the VM and configure it to run automatically when the VM starts. This might involve using a process manager like systemd or Supervisor. You can then access your application through the VM's public IP address or a domain name that you've configured to point to the VM. Load balancing can be configured to distribute traffic across multiple VM instances for high availability and scalability. Students often struggle with understanding the complexities of server administration. Providing clear instructions on how to connect to the VM, install software, configure web servers, and manage processes is crucial. Furthermore, emphasizing the importance of monitoring the deployed application's performance and logs is essential for identifying and resolving issues. By understanding the process of deploying Flask applications on AWS or GCP, students can gain valuable experience in managing cloud infrastructure and deploying scalable web applications.

Best Practices for Deployment

Deploying a Flask application is more than just getting it running on a server; it's about ensuring its reliability, scalability, security, and maintainability in a production environment. Following best practices is crucial for a smooth and successful deployment. Imagine you've built a Flask app that handles sensitive user data. Simply deploying it without considering security best practices could leave it vulnerable to attacks. As the Center for Internet Security (CIS) benchmarks emphasize, adhering to security best practices is paramount in any deployment scenario.

Several key areas should be considered when deploying a Flask application. Security is paramount. Use HTTPS to encrypt communication between the client and the server, protecting user data from interception. Implement robust authentication and authorization mechanisms to control access to your application's resources. Protect against common web vulnerabilities, such as cross-site scripting (XSS) and SQL injection, by properly validating and sanitizing user input. Regularly update your server's operating system and software to patch security vulnerabilities. A common question is how to choose the right authentication method. Consider using well-established authentication frameworks like OAuth or OpenID Connect for secure and standardized authentication. Avoid storing sensitive data, like passwords, in plain text; instead, use strong hashing algorithms to store password hashes.

Scalability is another important consideration. If you expect your application to handle a large volume of traffic, you need to design it to scale horizontally, meaning you can add more server instances to handle the load. Use a load balancer to distribute traffic across multiple instances of your application. Consider using caching mechanisms to reduce the load on your database and improve performance. Monitor your application's performance and resource usage to identify bottlenecks and optimize its scalability. A frequent question is how to choose the right load balancing strategy. Several strategies exist, such as round-robin, least connections, and IP hash. The choice depends on the specific requirements of your application and the traffic patterns. Load balancing is a complex topic, and understanding the trade-offs between different strategies is crucial for effective scaling.

Maintainability is also essential. Use a version control system like Git to track changes to your code and make deployment easier. Automate your deployment process using tools like CI/CD pipelines. This allows you to quickly and reliably deploy updates to your application. Use logging to track your application's behavior and identify issues. Monitor your application's health and performance using monitoring tools. A common question is why automation is so important. Automation reduces the risk of human error, speeds up the deployment process, and makes it easier to rollback changes if necessary. It also allows you to implement continuous integration and continuous deployment, enabling you to deploy updates more frequently and with greater confidence.

Finally, consider the specific requirements of your application. If your application uses a database, ensure that the database is properly configured and optimized. If your application uses external services, ensure that you have proper error handling and retry mechanisms in place. By following these best practices, including prioritizing security, designing for scalability, ensuring maintainability, and considering application-specific requirements, you can deploy your Flask applications effectively and confidently, knowing that they are robust, reliable, and secure. Students often struggle with understanding the complexities of scaling and securing web applications. Providing them with practical examples of how to implement these best practices, and explaining the trade-offs between different approaches, is crucial for preparing them for real-world deployment scenarios.

Chapter 13 Case Studies and Projects

Case Study 1: Predicting House Prices (Linear Regression)

Let's delve into a case study of predicting house prices using linear regression, a foundational machine learning technique. This scenario is highly relevant in real estate, finance, and urban planning, where accurate price estimations are crucial. Imagine a real estate company wanting to develop an automated system for valuing properties. They could use historical sales data, including features like square footage, number of bedrooms, location, and age of the house, to train a linear regression model. This model could then predict the price of new properties based on their features. As Draper and Smith (1998) explain in their work on applied regression analysis, linear regression provides a solid framework for modeling such relationships.[1]

The first step would involve data collection and preprocessing. The company would gather data on past house sales, ensuring data quality and consistency. This might involve cleaning the data to handle missing values, converting categorical variables (like location) into numerical representations (e.g., one-hot encoding), and potentially transforming numerical features (e.g., using logarithmic transformations for skewed data). Feature engineering might also be considered, creating new features from existing ones, such as the ratio of bedrooms to bathrooms or a combined score representing neighborhood quality. A common question is how to handle outliers in the data. Outliers, which are unusually high or low values, can significantly affect the linear regression model.[2] Techniques like removing outliers, transforming them, or using robust regression methods can mitigate their impact.[3]

Next, the data would be split into training and testing sets. The training set would be used to train the linear regression model, while the testing set would be used to evaluate its performance on unseen data. The linear regression model would then be trained using the training data, finding the coefficients that minimize the difference between the predicted and actual house prices. Scikit-learn in Python provides a convenient way to implement linear regression.[4] A frequent question is how to evaluate the model's performance. Several metrics can be used, such as Root Mean Squared Error (RMSE), Mean Absolute Error (MAE), and R-squared.[5] RMSE measures the average difference between the predicted and actual prices, MAE measures the average absolute difference, and R-squared measures the proportion of variance in house prices explained by the model. The choice of metric depends on the specific goals of the project.

Finally, the trained model could be deployed as part of a web application or integrated into the company's existing systems. Users could input the features of a new property, and the model would predict its price. The model could also be used to analyze market trends and identify factors that influence house prices. Students often struggle with understanding the assumptions of linear regression, such as linearity, independence of errors, homoscedasticity, and normality of errors.

Discussing these assumptions and how to check them using diagnostic plots and statistical tests, perhaps referencing Wooldridge (2016) on econometrics, is crucial. Furthermore, emphasizing the importance of interpreting the model's coefficients in the context of the problem and understanding the limitations of linear regression is essential for responsible use of the model. This case study provides a practical example of how linear regression can be applied to a real-world problem, from data collection and preprocessing to model training, evaluation, and deployment.

Case Study 2: Customer Segmentation (K-Means Clustering)

Let's explore a case study on customer segmentation using K-means clustering, a powerful unsupervised learning technique. This approach is widely used in marketing, retail, and customer relationship management (CRM) to understand customer behavior and personalize strategies. Imagine a retail company wanting to segment its customers based on their purchasing patterns. They could use K-means clustering to group customers with similar buying habits together, allowing them to target each segment with tailored marketing campaigns or product recommendations. As Jain (2010) discusses in his survey of clustering algorithms, K-means remains a popular and effective method for customer segmentation.

The first step involves data collection and preprocessing. The company would gather data on customer purchases, including information like purchase frequency, average order value, product categories purchased, and demographics. Data preprocessing would involve cleaning the data to handle missing values, scaling numerical features (e.g., using standardization or Min-Max scaling), and potentially encoding categorical variables. Feature engineering might also be considered, creating new features from existing ones, such as total spending or the number of different product categories purchased. A common question is how to handle high-dimensional data. Customer purchase data can be high-dimensional, especially if it includes a large number of products. Dimensionality reduction techniques like Principal

Component Analysis (PCA) can be used to reduce the number of features while preserving important information.

Next, the K-means clustering algorithm would be applied to the preprocessed data. The algorithm would partition the customers into k distinct clusters based on their similarity. The company would need to determine the optimal number of clusters k. The elbow method or the silhouette score can be used to help choose the appropriate k. The elbow method involves plotting the within-cluster sum of squares (WCSS) against k and looking for the "elbow" point. The silhouette score measures how similar a data point is to its own cluster compared to other clusters. A common question is how to interpret the resulting clusters. Once the customers are assigned to clusters, the company would analyze the characteristics of each cluster to understand the different customer segments. This might involve calculating summary statistics for each cluster, such as the average purchase frequency or the most popular product categories.

Finally, the customer segments can be used to personalize marketing strategies. For example, the company might offer targeted promotions to each segment, recommend products that are relevant to each segment's interests, or develop tailored communication strategies. The insights gained from customer segmentation can also be used to improve product development, customer service, and overall business strategy. Students often struggle with understanding the limitations of K-means clustering, such as its sensitivity to the initial centroid initialization and its assumption of spherical clusters. Discussing these limitations and alternative clustering algorithms, such as DBSCAN or hierarchical clustering, is crucial. Furthermore, emphasizing the importance of domain expertise in interpreting the clustering results and ensuring that the segments are meaningful and actionable is essential for effective customer segmentation. This case study provides a practical example of how K-means clustering can be applied to a real-world problem, from data collection and preprocessing to cluster analysis and marketing strategy development.

Case Study 3: Sentiment Analysis (Naive Bayes)

Let's explore a case study on sentiment analysis using Naive Bayes, a probabilistic classifier well-suited for text classification tasks. Sentiment analysis aims to determine the emotional tone or attitude expressed in a piece of text, whether it's positive, negative, or neutral.[1] This technique is invaluable in various domains, including social media monitoring, customer feedback analysis, and market research.[2] Imagine a company wanting to understand customer sentiment towards their new product by analyzing reviews posted online. Naive Bayes can be used to classify these reviews as positive, negative, or neutral, providing valuable insights into customer opinions.[3] As Rennie et al. (2003) demonstrate, Naive Bayes, despite its simplicity, can be surprisingly effective for text classification tasks like sentiment analysis.

The first step involves data collection and preprocessing. The company would gather a dataset of customer reviews, ensuring data quality and consistency. Preprocessing would involve cleaning the text data, which might include removing punctuation, converting text to lowercase, and handling special characters.[4] Tokenization, the process of splitting the text into individual words or phrases (tokens), is a crucial step.[5] Stop words, which are common words like "the," "a," and "is" that often don't carry much sentiment information, are typically removed.[6] Stemming or lemmatization, which reduces words to their root form (e.g., "running" to "run"), can also be helpful.[7] A common question is how to handle negations. Negations, like "not good," can flip the sentiment of a sentence.[8] Techniques like identifying negation words and modifying the subsequent words can help address this issue.

Next, the text data would be converted into a numerical representation that can be used by the Naive Bayes classifier. A common approach is to use bag-of-words or TF-IDF (Term Frequency-Inverse Document Frequency). Bag-of-words represents each review as a vector where each element corresponds to a word in the vocabulary, and the value represents the frequency of that word in[9] the review.[10] TF-IDF takes into account not only the frequency of a word in a review but also its importance across all reviews.[11] Scikit-learn provides tools like CountVectorizer and TfidfVectorizer to implement these techniques. A frequent question is how to choose between bag-of-words and TF-IDF. TF-IDF is generally preferred when the vocabulary is large, as it helps to downweight common words that might not be very informative.[12]

The Naive Bayes classifier would then be trained on the labeled reviews (reviews that have been manually labeled as positive, negative, or neutral). Scikit-learn provides classes like MultinomialNB (suitable for bag-of-words) and GaussianNB (suitable for continuous features, which can be derived from TF-IDF). The trained classifier can then be used to predict the sentiment of new, unseen reviews. A common question is how to evaluate the performance of the sentiment analysis model. Metrics like accuracy, precision, recall, and F1-score can be used. It's also important to consider the specific goals of the sentiment analysis task. For example, if it's more important to identify all negative reviews, even at the cost of some false positives, recall might be prioritized over precision. Students often struggle with understanding the naive assumption of feature independence in Naive Bayes. Explaining that while this assumption is often violated in real-world text data, Naive Bayes can still perform well due to its simplicity and efficiency, especially in high-dimensional spaces, is crucial. Furthermore, discussing the limitations of Naive Bayes, such as its sensitivity to zero probabilities and its inability to capture word order information, is essential. This case study provides a practical example of how Naive Bayes can be applied to a real-world problem like sentiment analysis, from data preprocessing and feature engineering to model training, evaluation, and interpretation.

Case Study 4: Image Classification (Neural Networks)

Let's explore a case study on image classification using neural networks, a powerful deep learning technique. Image classification aims to categorize images into predefined classes based on their visual content. This technology has wide-ranging applications, from medical diagnosis and object recognition to self-driving cars and security systems. Imagine a medical imaging company developing a system to automatically detect cancerous tumors in X-ray images. A neural network could be trained to classify X-ray images as containing a tumor or not, assisting radiologists in making faster and more accurate diagnoses. As LeCun et al. (2015) demonstrate, deep learning has revolutionized image classification, achieving human-level performance on some tasks.

The first step involves data collection and preprocessing. The company would gather a large dataset of X-ray images, ensuring data quality and consistency. Each image would be labeled with the corresponding diagnosis (tumor or no tumor). Preprocessing would involve resizing the images to a consistent size, normalizing pixel values (e.g., scaling pixel values to be between 0 and 1), and potentially augmenting the data. Data augmentation involves applying transformations to existing images, such as rotations, flips, or zooms, to create new training examples. This increases the diversity of the training data and helps the network generalize better. A common question is how to handle imbalanced datasets, where one class has significantly more examples than the other. Techniques like oversampling the minority class, undersampling the majority class, or using weighted loss functions can help address this issue.

Next, a suitable neural network architecture would be chosen. Convolutional Neural Networks (CNNs) are particularly well-suited for image classification tasks due to their ability to learn spatial hierarchies of features. A typical CNN architecture consists of convolutional layers, pooling layers, and fully connected layers. Convolutional layers learn to detect features like edges and textures, pooling layers reduce the spatial dimensions of the feature maps, and fully connected layers combine the learned features to make a classification decision. Pre-trained models, which have been trained on large datasets like ImageNet, can be used as a starting point and fine-tuned on the specific medical image dataset. This technique, known as transfer learning, can significantly reduce training time and improve performance, especially when the dataset is relatively small. A frequent question is how to choose the right CNN architecture. Several architectures exist, such as ResNet, VGG, and Inception. The choice often depends on the complexity of the task and the available computational resources.

The chosen CNN would then be trained on the labeled X-ray images. The network would learn to adjust its weights to minimize the difference between its predictions and the actual diagnoses. The training process typically involves using an optimization algorithm like Adam and a loss function like categorical cross-entropy. The performance of the trained network would be evaluated on a separate test set to assess its generalization ability. Metrics like accuracy, precision, recall, and F1-score can be used. A common question is how to interpret the results and identify potential issues. Visualizing the network's learned features or using techniques like Grad-CAM can help understand which parts of the image are most influential in the classification decision. Students often struggle with understanding the concept of backpropagation and how it works. Explaining the chain rule of calculus and how it is used to calculate gradients and update the network's weights can clarify this concept. Furthermore, discussing the challenges of training deep neural networks, such as vanishing gradients and overfitting, and techniques to address these challenges, such as batch normalization and dropout, is essential. This case study provides a practical example of how neural networks can be applied to a real-world problem like medical image classification, from data preprocessing and model selection to training, evaluation, and interpretation.

Part 5 Appendices and Resources

Appendix A: Python Cheat Sheet

Python Syntax and Libraries

Python's clear syntax and extensive libraries contribute significantly to its popularity in data science, machine learning, and web development. A solid understanding of core Python syntax and familiarity with key libraries are essential for any aspiring data scientist or web developer. This cheat sheet provides a concise overview of these fundamental elements, serving as a quick reference during development. Imagine you're working on a data analysis project. You might need to quickly recall the syntax for list comprehensions or remember how to use the Pandas library to manipulate DataFrames. This cheat sheet aims to provide that readily accessible information. As Van Rossum and Drake (2009) explain in "Python 3 Reference Manual," the language's design emphasizes readability and ease of use, which is reflected in its straightforward syntax.

Python syntax emphasizes readability through indentation. Code blocks are defined by consistent indentation, typically four spaces. This eliminates the need for curly braces or other delimiters, making the code cleaner and easier to read. Data types include integers, floating-point numbers, strings, booleans, lists, tuples, and dictionaries. Lists are mutable sequences of items, while tuples are immutable. Dictionaries are key-value pairs. Control flow statements include if, elif, else for conditional execution, for and while for looping, and break and continue for controlling loop execution. Functions are defined using the def keyword and can accept arguments and return values. A common question is how to handle exceptions. Python uses try, except, and finally blocks for exception handling. The try block contains the code that might raise an exception, the except block handles specific exceptions, and the finally block contains code that is always executed, regardless of whether an exception occurred.

Python's standard library provides a wealth of modules for various tasks. For data manipulation and analysis, Pandas is a crucial library. It provides DataFrames, which are two-dimensional labeled data structures, and functions for reading and writing data in various formats (CSV, Excel, etc.). NumPy is another essential library for numerical computing. It provides arrays and matrices, along with functions for mathematical operations, linear algebra, and random number generation. For data visualization, Matplotlib and Seaborn are widely used libraries. Matplotlib provides a low-level interface for creating various types of plots, while Seaborn builds on top of Matplotlib to provide a higher-level interface for creating statistically informative and visually appealing plots. A frequent question is how to install and manage libraries. Python uses pip, the package installer, for this purpose. You can install a library using pip install library_name and list installed libraries using pip list. Creating a requirements.txt file to list project dependencies is a best practice for managing and reproducing project environments.

For web development, Flask is a popular microframework. It provides tools for routing, templating, and handling HTTP requests. For machine learning, scikit-learn provides a wide range of algorithms for classification, regression, clustering, and dimensionality reduction. TensorFlow and PyTorch are popular deep learning libraries. They provide tools for building and training neural networks. Students often struggle with remembering the specific syntax or function names. Using online documentation, interactive Python interpreters, and regularly practicing coding exercises are helpful strategies. Furthermore, understanding the underlying concepts and principles is more important than memorizing specific syntax. By understanding the core syntax and becoming familiar with commonly used libraries, developers can efficiently leverage Python's capabilities for a wide range of tasks.

Common Pandas and NumPy Operations

Pandas and NumPy are fundamental libraries in the Python data science ecosystem, providing powerful tools for data manipulation and numerical computation. A solid understanding of common operations in these libraries is crucial for any data scientist. This cheat sheet summarizes frequently used operations, serving as a quick reference during data analysis and model building. Imagine you're working on a project to analyze sales data. You might need to quickly filter data in a Pandas DataFrame, calculate summary statistics, or perform array operations using NumPy. This cheat sheet aims to provide a concise reminder of these essential operations. As McKinney (2010) explains in his book on data structures and algorithms with Pandas, mastering these libraries is key to efficient data analysis in Python.

Pandas DataFrames are the workhorse of data manipulation. Creating a DataFrame can be done from various data sources, including CSV files, dictionaries, and lists. Indexing and selecting data can be achieved using labels (.loc) or integer positions (.iloc). Filtering data based on conditions is a common operation. For example, you might want to select all rows where a specific column value is greater than a certain threshold. This can be done using boolean indexing. Adding new columns or modifying existing ones is also straightforward. You can apply functions to columns using .apply() or .map(). Grouping and aggregating data is another powerful feature. You can group data by one or more columns and then calculate summary statistics (e.g., mean, sum, count) for each group. A common question is how to handle missing data. Pandas provides functions like .fillna() to fill missing values and .dropna() to remove rows or columns with missing values. Choosing the appropriate method for handling missing data depends on the specific context and the nature of the data.

NumPy arrays are essential for numerical computations. Creating arrays can be done from lists or using functions like np.array(), np.zeros(), np.ones(), and np.arange(). Array operations are performed element-wise by default. For example, adding two arrays will add the corresponding elements. Broadcasting allows operations between arrays of different shapes under certain conditions. Slicing and indexing arrays is similar to Python lists. You can select specific elements or subarrays using indexing and slicing. Reshaping arrays can be done using np.reshape(). This is often necessary when working with machine learning models that expect data in a specific format. A frequent question is how to perform matrix operations. NumPy provides functions for matrix multiplication (np.dot() or @ operator), transpose (.T), and inverse (np.linalg.inv()). Linear algebra operations are crucial for many machine learning algorithms.

Combining Pandas and NumPy is often necessary. You can access the underlying NumPy array of a Pandas Series or DataFrame using .values. This allows you to leverage NumPy's efficient array operations on Pandas data structures. Students often struggle with understanding the difference between Pandas Series and DataFrames. Explaining that a Series is a one-dimensional labeled array, while a DataFrame is a two-dimensional labeled data structure, like a table, can clarify this concept. Furthermore, practicing with real-world datasets and exploring the extensive documentation of both libraries is crucial for mastering these tools. By understanding these common Pandas and NumPy operations, data scientists can efficiently manipulate and analyze data, laying the foundation for building effective machine learning models and web applications.

Appendix B: Machine Learning Cheat Sheet

Overview of Algorithms

This machine learning cheat sheet provides a concise overview of common algorithms, categorized by learning paradigm (supervised, unsupervised, and reinforcement learning). It's designed as a quick reference for students and practitioners, helping them choose the appropriate algorithm for a given task. Imagine you're faced with a new machine learning problem. This cheat sheet can serve as a starting point, reminding you of the different algorithms available and their key characteristics. As James et al. (2013) discuss in their book on statistical learning, understanding the strengths and weaknesses of different algorithms is essential for effective model selection.

Supervised Learning: This paradigm involves learning from labeled data, where both input features and corresponding target values are provided.

- **Regression:** Predicting a continuous target variable.
  - o **Linear Regression:** Assumes a linear relationship between features and the target. Simple to implement and interpret but assumes linearity.
  - o **Polynomial Regression:** Extends linear regression to model non-linear relationships using polynomial features. Captures non-linearity but can overfit.

- o **Support Vector Regression (SVR):** Uses kernel trick to model non-linear relationships in high-dimensional spaces. Effective in high dimensions but computationally expensive.

- o **Decision Tree Regression:** Partitions the data space into smaller regions based on feature values. Easy to interpret but can overfit.

- o **Random Forest Regression:** Combines multiple decision trees to improve accuracy and robustness. Reduces overfitting but less interpretable.

- **Classification:** Predicting a categorical target variable.
  - o **Logistic Regression:** Predicts the probability of a class using a sigmoid function. Simple and efficient for binary classification.

  - o **Support Vector Machines (SVM):** Finds the optimal hyperplane to separate classes. Effective in high dimensions but computationally expensive.

  - o **K-Nearest Neighbors (KNN):** Classifies data points based on the majority class among their k-nearest neighbors. Simple but computationally expensive for large datasets.

  - o **Decision Tree Classification:** Similar to decision tree regression, but predicts a class label. Easy to interpret but can overfit.

  - o **Random Forest Classification:** Combines multiple decision trees for classification. Reduces overfitting but less interpretable.

- o **Naive Bayes:** A probabilistic classifier based on Bayes' theorem. Efficient for text classification.

- o **Neural Networks:** Complex models with multiple layers that can learn complex patterns. Powerful but require large datasets and computational resources.

Unsupervised Learning: This paradigm involves learning from unlabeled data, where only input features are provided.

- **Clustering:** Grouping similar data points together.

  - o **K-Means Clustering:** Partitions data points into k clusters based on their distance to centroids. Simple and efficient but assumes spherical clusters.

  - o **Hierarchical Clustering:** Builds a hierarchy of clusters. Can be agglomerative (bottom-up) or divisive (top-down). Provides a dendrogram for visualization.

  - o **DBSCAN:** Identifies clusters based on density. Robust to outliers and can discover clusters of arbitrary shapes.

- **Dimensionality Reduction:** Reducing the number of features while preserving important information.

  - o **Principal Component Analysis (PCA):** Finds the principal components that capture the most variance in the data. Reduces dimensionality and can be used for feature extraction.

  - o **t-SNE:** Visualizes high-dimensional data in low dimensions. Useful for exploring data but can distort distances.

- **Association Rule Learning:** Discovering relationships between variables.

o **Apriori:** Finds frequent itemsets and association rules. Used in market basket analysis.

Reinforcement Learning: This paradigm involves an agent learning to interact with an environment by taking actions and receiving rewards or penalties.

- **Q-Learning:** Learns a Q-value function that estimates the optimal action to take in a given state. Model-free and can handle stochastic environments.

- **SARSA:** Similar to Q-learning but updates the Q-value function based on the actual action taken. On-policy and can be more stable.

- **Deep Reinforcement Learning:** Combines reinforcement learning with deep neural networks. Can handle complex environments and high-dimensional state spaces.

Students often struggle with choosing the appropriate algorithm for a given problem. Emphasizing the importance of considering the type of data, the goal of the task, and the trade-offs between different algorithms is crucial. Furthermore, understanding the assumptions and limitations of each algorithm is essential for responsible use. This cheat sheet provides a starting point for exploring the world of machine learning algorithms. Further research and experimentation are necessary for mastering these techniques.

Key Parameters and Use Cases

This section of the Python cheat sheet focuses on key parameters and use cases for common Python libraries used in data science and machine learning. Understanding the parameters of functions and classes within libraries like Pandas, NumPy, scikit-learn, and others is crucial for effectively utilizing these tools. Knowing the typical use cases helps in applying the right tool for the job. Imagine you're working on a data preprocessing step. Knowing the parameters of the StandardScaler in scikit-learn will allow you to correctly scale your data. Similarly, understanding the use cases for different classification algorithms will help you select the most appropriate one for your task. As the documentation for these libraries emphasize, familiarity with parameters and use cases is essential for effective data analysis and model building.

Pandas:

- **pd.read_csv()**: Key parameters include filepath_or_buffer (path to the CSV file), sep (delimiter), header (row number for header), index_col (column to use as index), and usecols (columns to read). Use case: Reading data from CSV files into a DataFrame.

- **DataFrame.groupby()**: Key parameters include by (columns to group by), axis (0 for rows, 1 for columns), and agg (aggregation function). Use case: Grouping data for aggregation and analysis.

- **DataFrame.fillna()**: Key parameter value (value to fill missing values with). Use case: Handling missing data.

-

NumPy:

- **np.array():** Key parameter object (the array-like object to create the array from). Use case: Creating NumPy arrays.

- **np.zeros()/np.ones():** Key parameter shape (shape of the array). Use case: Creating arrays of zeros or ones.

- **np.linspace():** Key parameters start, stop, and num (number of evenly spaced samples). Use case: Creating evenly spaced arrays.

Scikit-learn:

- **StandardScaler():** Key parameter with_mean and with_std (whether to center and scale). Use case: Scaling numerical features.

- **LinearRegression():** Key parameter fit_intercept (whether to calculate the intercept). Use case: Linear regression.

- **LogisticRegression():** Key parameters penalty (regularization), C (inverse of regularization strength), and solver (optimization algorithm). Use case: Logistic regression for classification.

- **KMeans():** Key parameter n_clusters (number of clusters). Use case: K-means clustering.

- **train_test_split():** Key parameters arrays (data arrays), test_size (size of the test set), and random_state (random seed). Use case: Splitting data into training and testing sets.

Other Libraries:

- **Matplotlib:** plt.plot() key parameters x, y, linestyle, marker, label. Use case: Plotting data.

- **Seaborn:** sns.scatterplot() key parameters x, y, hue, data. Use case: Creating scatter plots.

Students often struggle with understanding the impact of different parameter values. Providing clear examples of how changing parameter values affects the output of functions and classes is crucial. Furthermore, encouraging students to explore the documentation of these libraries and experiment with different parameter settings is essential for developing a deeper understanding of these tools. This section of the cheat sheet serves as a starting point for exploring the world of Python's data science libraries. Consistent practice and exploration of the documentation are key to mastering these powerful tools.

Appendix C: Flask Cheat Sheet

Flask Basics and Common Patterns

This Flask cheat sheet provides a concise overview of Flask basics and common patterns for web development. It's designed as a quick reference for students and practitioners building web applications with Flask. Imagine you're developing a simple web application to display data from a database. You might need to quickly recall how to define routes, render templates, or handle form submissions. This cheat sheet aims to provide that readily accessible information. As Grinberg (2018) explains in his book on Flask web development, understanding these basics is essential for building robust and maintainable Flask applications.

Flask Basics:

- **Creating a Flask app:** from flask import Flask; app = Flask(__name__) initializes a Flask application.

- **Defining routes:** @app.route("/") decorates a function to handle requests to the root URL. You can also define dynamic routes: @app.route("/user/<username>").

- **Running the development server:** app.run(debug=True) starts the development server. The debug=True option enables automatic reloading and debugging.

- **Handling requests:** from flask import request; request.form accesses submitted form data. request.args accesses URL query parameters.

- **Rendering templates:** from flask import render_template; return render_template("index.html", name=name) renders the index.html template, passing the name variable.

- **Redirecting:** from flask import redirect, url_for; return redirect(url_for("index")) redirects the user to the URL associated with the index function.

- **Flash messages:** from flask import flash; flash("Message") adds a message to the flash. In the template, use {% with messages = get_flashed_messages() %} and {% for message in messages %} to display flashed messages.

Common Patterns:

- **Blueprints:** Organizing larger applications into smaller, reusable components. from flask import Blueprint; my_blueprint = Blueprint("my_blueprint", __name__); app.register_blueprint(my_blueprint)

- **Database interaction:** Using SQLAlchemy or other database libraries to interact with databases. Define models and use ORM functionalities.

- **Form handling:** Using WTForms or similar libraries to define and handle forms. Validate user input and display error messages.

- **Authentication and authorization:** Implementing user authentication and authorization using Flask extensions like Flask-Login or Flask-Security.

- **Handling static files:** Serving static files (CSS, JavaScript, images) from a static directory. Use url_for('static', filename='style.css') in templates.

- **Error handling:** Using try-except blocks to handle potential errors and display user-friendly error messages.

- **Testing:** Writing unit tests for your Flask application using the flask.testing module or other testing frameworks like pytest.

Key Considerations:

- **Security:** Always use HTTPS. Protect against common web vulnerabilities like XSS and SQL injection. Implement proper authentication and authorization.

- **Deployment:** Use a production-ready WSGI server like Gunicorn or uWSGI. Deploy to a platform like Heroku, AWS, or Google Cloud.

- **Scalability:** Design your application to scale horizontally if needed. Use load balancers and caching mechanisms.

Students often struggle with understanding how to structure larger Flask applications. Emphasizing the use of blueprints for modularity and explaining how to organize templates and static files is crucial. Furthermore, discussing the importance of security best practices and providing examples of how to implement them is essential for responsible web development. This cheat sheet serves as a quick reference. Exploring the official Flask documentation and working through tutorials are highly recommended for a deeper understanding.

Deployment Checklist

Deploying a Flask application involves more than just copying files to a server; it requires careful planning and execution to ensure a smooth transition from development to production. A deployment checklist helps to organize the process and avoid common pitfalls. Imagine you've built a Flask application that predicts traffic patterns. Simply uploading the code to a server without proper configuration could lead to security vulnerabilities, performance issues, and downtime. A checklist ensures you've considered all aspects of the deployment, from security to scalability. As Grinberg (2018) emphasizes, a well-defined deployment process is crucial for the success of any web application.

A comprehensive deployment checklist should cover several key areas. **Environment Preparation:** First, ensure the server environment mirrors your development environment as closely as possible. This includes installing the correct Python version and all required dependencies. Use a requirements.txt file to manage dependencies and avoid version conflicts. Create a virtual environment on the server to isolate your application's dependencies. A common question is why a virtual environment is necessary on the server. It ensures that the server has the exact same dependencies as your development environment, preventing unexpected errors due to missing or conflicting packages.

Application Configuration: Next, configure your Flask application for production. Disable debugging mode (debug=False) to prevent sensitive information from being exposed. Set up environment variables for sensitive data, such as database credentials or API keys.

Never hardcode these values directly in your code. A frequent question is how to manage environment variables on the server. Different hosting providers offer different ways to set environment variables. Consult the documentation for your chosen platform.

Web Server and Reverse Proxy: Choose a production-ready WSGI server like Gunicorn or uWSGI. These servers are more efficient and secure than the Flask development server. Configure a reverse proxy like Nginx or Apache to sit in front of your WSGI server. The reverse proxy handles static files, load balancing, and SSL termination. A common question is why a reverse proxy is needed. It improves performance by caching static files and handling multiple requests efficiently. It also enhances security by hiding the WSGI server from the outside world.

Database and Static Files: If your application uses a database, ensure it's properly configured and accessible from the server. Back up your database before deployment. Organize your static files (CSS, JavaScript, images) in a static directory and configure your web server to serve them efficiently. A frequent question is how to handle database migrations. Use a database migration tool like Alembic to manage database schema changes. This ensures that your database schema is consistent across different environments.

Security: Implement HTTPS to encrypt communication between the client and the server. Configure firewalls to restrict access to your server. Regularly update your server's operating system and software to patch security vulnerabilities. A common question is how to obtain an SSL certificate. You can obtain free SSL certificates from Let's Encrypt or purchase them from a commercial certificate authority.

Monitoring and Logging: Set up logging to track your application's behavior and identify errors. Use a monitoring tool to monitor your server's resources (CPU, memory, disk space) and application performance. A frequent question is how to choose the right monitoring tools. Several options exist, from simple log analysis tools to sophisticated monitoring platforms. The choice depends on the complexity of your application and your monitoring needs.

Testing and Deployment Process: Thoroughly test your application in a staging environment before deploying it to production. Automate your deployment process using tools like CI/CD pipelines. This makes deployments faster, more reliable, and easier to rollback if necessary. Students often struggle with understanding the importance of testing in a staging environment. Explaining that it allows you to catch errors before they affect users in the production environment is crucial. This deployment checklist provides a framework for a successful deployment. Remember to adapt it to your specific application and hosting environment. Thorough planning and attention to detail are key to a smooth and trouble-free deployment.

Bibliography

[1] Agresti, A. (2015). *Foundations of Linear and Generalized Linear Models.* Wiley.

[2] Beazley, D. M. (2013). *Python Essential Reference.* Addison-Wesley.

[3] Bolton, R. J., & Hand, D. J. (2002). *Statistical Fraud Detection: A Review.* Statistical Science, 17(3), 235–255.

[4] Breiman, L. (2001). *Random Forests.* Machine Learning, 45(1), 5–32.

[5] Breiman, L., Friedman, J., Olshen, R., & Stone, C. (1984). *Classification and Regression Trees.* CRC Press.

[6] Buolamwini, J., & Gebru, T. (2018). *Gender Shades: Intersectional Accuracy Disparities in Commercial Gender Classification.* Proceedings of Machine Learning Research, 81, 1–15.

[7] Chen, M., Mao, S., & Liu, Y. (2015). *Big Data: A Survey.* Mobile Networks and Applications, 19(2), 171–209.

[8] Cortes, C., & Vapnik, V. (1995). *Support-Vector Networks.* Machine Learning, 20(3), 273–297.

[9] Draper, N. R., & Smith, H. (1998). *Applied Regression Analysis.* Wiley.

[10] Gomez-Uribe, C. A., & Hunt, N. (2015). *The Netflix Recommender System: Algorithms, Business Value, and Innovation.* ACM Transactions on Management Information Systems, 6(4), 1–19.

[11] Goodfellow, I., Bengio, Y., & Courville, A. (2016). *Deep Learning.* MIT Press.

[12] Harris, C. R., Millman, K. J., van der Walt, S. J., et al. (2020). *Array Programming with NumPy.* Nature, 585(7825), 357–362.

[13] Hastie, T., Tibshirani, R., & Friedman, J. (2009). *The Elements of Statistical Learning: Data Mining, Inference, and Prediction.* Springer.

[14] Hosmer, D. W., & Lemeshow, S. (2000). *Applied Logistic Regression.* Wiley.

[15] Jordan, M. I., & Mitchell, T. M. (2015). *Machine Learning: Trends, Perspectives, and Prospects.* Science, 349(6245), 255–260.

[16] Linden, G., Smith, B., & York, J. (2003). *Amazon.com Recommendations: Item-to-Item Collaborative Filtering.* IEEE Internet Computing, 7(1), 76–80.

[17] Little, R. J. A., & Rubin, D. B. (2019). *Statistical Analysis with Missing Data.* Wiley.

[18] Provost, F., & Kohavi, R. (1998). *Guest Editors' Introduction: On Applied Research in Machine Learning.* Machine Learning, 30(2/3), 127–132.

[19] Sutton, R. S., & Barto, A. G. (2018). *Reinforcement Learning: An Introduction.* MIT Press.

[20] Wickham, H. (2014). *Tidy Data.* Journal of Statistical Software, 59(10), 1–23.

About The Author

Mark John Lado is a Filipino technology and education professional with a deep passion for advancing knowledge and innovation in the fields of Information Systems and Technology Education. An accomplished Information System Specialist, Mark excels in areas such as Object-Oriented Programming (OOP), Teacher Mentoring, Computer Hardware, Software System Analysis, and Web Development. He earned his Master's degree in Information Technology from Northern Negros State College of Science and Technology in Sagay City, Philippines, and is currently pursuing his Doctorate in Information Technology at the State University of Northern Negros.

Mark has built a diverse career in education, holding various teaching and administrative roles. Currently, he is an Instructor in the College of Technology and Engineering at Cebu Technological University, San Francisco, Camotes Campus, where he has been serving since October 2022. Prior to this, he was a Faculty member in Business Education and Information Systems at Colegio de San Antonio de Padua from 2018 to 2022. He also worked as a Part-Time Information Technology Instructor at the University of the Visayas - Danao Branch in 2017 and as an ICT Coordinator at Carmen Christian School Inc. during the same period.

A lifelong learner, Mark has pursued several certifications, including Computer Hardware Servicing from Cebu Technological University and Consumer Electronics Servicing from TESDA, showcasing his commitment to continuous professional development.

Mark is an active member of the Philippine Society of Information Technology Educators (PSITE), where he contributes to advancing the standards of IT education in the Philippines. His research work reflects his dedication to innovation, with notable projects including "Development of a Microprocessor-Based Sensor Network for Monitoring Water Parameters in Tilapia Traponds" and "A Wireless Digital Public Address with Voice Alarm and Text-to-Speech Feature for Different Campuses," which was published in Globus: An International Journal of Management & IT.

Beyond his teaching and research endeavors, Mark has authored and published multiple books on various technology topics, including PC troubleshooting, operating systems, embedded systems, and data modeling. While many of his key works are widely recognized, additional publications showcasing his expertise are available on his Amazon author page.

Mark's dedication to education, research, and professional excellence, combined with his adaptability to emerging technological trends, has made him a respected figure in the academic and IT communities. His unwavering passion for technology and his continuous pursuit of learning ensure his valuable contributions to the development of future IT professionals.

Biography Source:

Mark John Lado. (n.d.). Biographies.net. Retrieved January 24, 2025, from https://www.biographies.net/

Authors' Official Website:

https://markjohnlado.com/

www.ingramcontent.com/pod-product-compliance
Lightning Source LLC
LaVergne TN
LVHW051335050326
832903LV00031B/3548